MAN'S
SEARCH
FOR
HAPPINESS

MAN'S SEARCH FOR HAPPINESS

ASHWIN SUNDER

SHY CAT PUBLICATIONS
SAN FRANCISCO

ISBN (print) 978-1-71028-529-1

Cover design by Gabanelli Marco
Formatting by Gabanelli Marco
Editing by Maiyone Zelph

Printed in the United States of America

For all men

Contents

Introduction

Man's desperate pursuit of happiness has been the single greatest source of evil throughout the ages. All men strive frantically to be eternally happy. And in this pursuit they fail continually. From the ensuing misery, arises the potential and the fact of great evil, both interpersonal and on a global scale. History is rife with much needless suffering in the form of both self-inflicted misery and the misery that man has wrought upon his fellow human beings. And yet, the modern man's needy preoccupation with himself and with securing the concept of happiness for himself has taken this evil to even newer heights.

No animal can exist in a state of eternal happiness. The twin desires of survival of its flesh and maximal propagation of its genes compel it to wander restlessly in search of rewards. Yet when those rewards are at hand, there is no celebration, mere relief at best. New goals are sighted and the creature resumes its search, destroying everything that it thinks gets in its way. As animals at the core, humans form no exception to this condition. To make matters worse, as thinking beings with a vibrant conception of the self, we can contemplate our misery in depth and struggle against the bounds, but in vain. The many constraints of life then form the basis of a new kind of unhappiness. This is the fundamental human condition, and it preoccupies the mind at all times.

Once upon a time, a primeval creature lived in a cave, on a tree branch, or under the stars. This early human animal had a limited conception of its condition. When sleep came, it laid down. When hunger came, it ate. For this it hunted other creatures or scrounged sustenance from the land. At times this creature failed to satisfy its needs. It suffered from hunger, thirst, disease, injury, or other deprivations. It saw others around itself grow old or die young, and eventually it too died. It may have erupted in rudimentary laughter and crying, but it had no words for its happiness. It did not know that it should actively seek out this happiness as a separate thing. Everything was experienced as is.

Now man does have a word for it. Happy. The word itself derives from 'happenstance' and originally denoted good luck, rather than an emotional state. Placing one's faith on rolling the dice and hoping to get lucky seems like a bad idea on how to live life, yet that is exactly how modern man lives, as he continually pursues peak positive experiences without realizing that he is no different from a gambling addict chasing the highs. The ancients emphasized the value of all emotions, positive and negative, but that message was lost somewhere along the line to modernity. The unrelenting quest for his own happiness is now man's primary and all encompassing obsession, and it comes at the cost of precisely that.

The pursuit of happiness. Who can deny any man that right? Man has written books about it, he has it enshrined in the constitution, and he encounters the concept everywhere he turns, whether stated or unstated. Ask someone why they do anything, and you will get a shrug and a statement to the effect that it just makes them happy. Something has been created out of nothing. And man spends his entire life pursuing this elusive nothingness. It is as though there was something that he was supposed to find and keep in his possession, and it has temporarily gone missing. And it is this constant pursuit in itself that becomes a source of man's misery.

What exactly is happiness? For all his obsession about it, man does not even know what the word really means. His dictionary helpfully defines it as the state of being happy. Psychologists stumble and repeat words when they define happiness as a generally positive mood or emotional state brought about in turn by generally positive thoughts or feelings. Being happy is clearly an overloaded term. There are many approaches that only hint at how one arrives at a state of being happy. One could say that being happy means having fond memories of one's past, joy in the present moment, and a positive outlook for one's future. One could say that happiness is not about fleeting pleasures but about contentment with one's life and life purpose. Perhaps one robust definition of happiness could be that it is a state of not being unhappy. There are a million ways and reasons for being unhappy, and as anyone who is unhappy will vouch, they would rather talk about which one of those million things they don't have that makes them unhappy, than talk about what they have for which they are happy.

Whatever be the slippery nature of the notion of happiness, perhaps we need not concern ourselves with an exact definition. This book is not a guide on how and where to seek happiness. Of course, there are a few broad and obvious avenues where man wanders long and earnestly, with varying amounts of success. Sometimes he is rewarded with some satisfaction, and other times he turns even deeper into despair. Laying out a big map that charts his route to happiness is not the ultimate point of the book. On the contrary, this book is about how to escape that search altogether. The opposite of a search for happiness is not a search for unhappiness, and in any case, man needs no special instruction in that regard. The opposite of an endless search for happiness is a cessation of that fruitless seeking, and that is the state of being that this book aspires for man to reach.

The text is divided into two parts. In the first part, we will examine twelve aspects of life in which man typically searches for his happiness. These are the usual and familiar and yet highly debated sources of satisfaction, such as wealth, success, love and faith. We will consider what aids him and what fails him in these aspects. We will contrast man's current condition with that of primitive man, and see how things have changed over the eons. In all our examination of the typical places where happiness is sought, there may admittedly not be a single original idea. This is to be expected given the age old nature of the problem that has endlessly tortured all philosophers of life. The human condition has always existed alongside man and always will.

In the second part of this book, we will draw upon wisdom, ancient and modern, regarding why man feels the way he does, as seen in the context of the major milestones of birth and death. We will unearth the root cause of man's misery, and discuss as well the self-destructive manner in which man seeks relief from his condition, thus giving rise to evil and even more misery. Finally, we will offer a chance at a rebirth of one's perspectives on happiness, with a line of thinking that rejects the modern obsession with happiness and seeks to revert to a more natural and primeval mental state of being. Adopting this mental state may not be easy or to everyone's preference. Indeed, an initial reading of the topics in this book may likely make one feel discontent and distressed for an indefinite period. In the end though, a full and thorough assimilation of the ideas contained here will prove deeply superior to the commonly prevailing attitudes in modern society about happiness.

A note about a choice made in writing this book. Throughout the text, the word man along with the pronoun he are used to refer to an individual human. There are a few reasons for this choice. Firstly, it is to simplify the act of reading. Rather than to say he or she each time or to switch genders back and forth, we can just understand that man and he in the text generally stand for all humans, male or female, without any loss of meaning to the message conveyed. In a few situations where reference needs to be made specifically to the male or female gender, that is duly done, or else the context should make it obvious.

Secondly, it is simply a matter of subject matter expertise for the author. Men and women are very similar in the sense that they are both human beings, but they are not alike. When two separate things are very similar, it is the small differences that matter. That men and women ought to have equal rights and privileges does not imply that they have the exact same desires and drives. Anything that is stated about a gender different from one's own can only be inferred or hearsay, not experienced. The author can only claim firsthand knowledge and acquaintance with the thoughts of his own gender. Thus, the book is written by a man, for men. Much of its contents may of course apply to women as well, but that is not a claim made aforehand.

A final reason, and perhaps the strongest one, is that the use of man to represent humanity is simply more appropriate to the narrative of this book. Throughout all of history, men have enacted a far, far greater share of all evil acts committed, especially at the extremes of evil. Murderers, genocidal mass murderers, serial killers, criminals, warmongers, psychopaths, frauds, despots and tyrants are almost overwhelmingly male. Of course, men are also capable of incredible acts of kindness and good, have done much heavy lifting to progress humanity. Women too are far from perfect themselves, and suffer from much of the same flaws as men do. This does not change the facts, that the evil that men do is clearly far out of proportion to their numbers. There is good reason then, to address man directly in this text, and to call him out specifically. If man is a beast, then in trying frantically to claim the happiness he believes he is entitled to, he becomes an even bigger beast.

This is the book of the modern beast.

PART I.

THE ETERNAL SEARCH

Sugar

Death for one creature is merely dinner for another.

- Anonymous

No man can love God, his country, or his neighbor on an empty stomach.

- Woodrow Wilson

Man claims to be the most cultured and evolved of all creatures, standing apart from the other species. Yet, every few hours, he must make an obscene admission to his own animal nature by chomping down gluttonously on the flesh of other creatures, plant or animal. His body is a needy creature with an endless appetite for food, sleep and comforting. Of these, food is perhaps the most persistent and nagging need. At least when man is asleep, he is asleep. Sleep comes naturally and then one is dead to the world for a few hours. Hunger strikes man when he is at peak awareness, in the embarrassingly bright hours of the day. It is that incessant and annoying demand that arises in his belly and makes its way to his thoughts, always surprising him when he is in the midst of doing something important. It doesn't matter how tough or strong willed is a man, his hunger will always win out, and remind him of his chief and glaring limitation. His blood's pathetic need for regular infusions of sugar.

Every day, man must kill and consume yet another living thing, piece by piece, for his own continued survival. No other daily activity that he engages in carries quite the same burden of guilt as food. This is his curse for being the only animal to have evolved both consciousness and a conscience. No amount of obfuscation can hide this fact, even though he tries his damndest by consuming the most culturally refined, sophisticated and elegant dishes he can prepare. He can dress his food up as carefully as he wishes, with beautiful colors, shapes, textures and smells, but there is no escaping the stark conclusion. What was once a life form is now mere fuel that enters through the mouth and is excreted as waste through the anus. Over his entire lifetime, he will have gorged with delight on the remains of thousands of countless souls who once lived and thrived too.

Given this sombre realization, it is a great compensating fact that nature has programmed man to derive much pleasure and satisfaction from the act of consumption. Of course, food is not simply an idle luxury. With his belly full, with sugar coursing through his body, man can talk, he can walk, he can play. He can make love or make war. He build or destroy as he wishes. He can climb mountains and chart the oceans and explore his world. He can attain the heights of artistic creation. He can accumulate riches and power. And he can propagate his species. Take his food away though, and inevitably, within a matter of a few days, all men are reduced to desperate hungry savages with that one thing on their minds. How to saturate their blood once more with that precious sugar.

With the sole exception of the flesh of seed-bearing fruits, no creature wants itself or its parts to be eaten. All plants and animals put up a variety of defenses against becoming food, but man in his cleverness has developed elaborate mechanisms to circumvent all of these. He goes a step further even, by denying the unwillingness of other life to become food. Whether it is the smiling pigs on the cover of a pack of sausage or the happily grazing cows in a beef commercial, in all of his cheery advertisements of food, those being eaten are shown as fortunate, happy creatures, at times even inviting man to take a bite. This laughable fantasy is a recent invention of modern society. Any hunter who had to take down an animal or any farmer who had to butcher his own livestock would think differently of such portrayals. Since man today rarely wields the knife himself, he can be made to believe, even slightly at that little instant that he picks his food out from the supermarket shelf, that there is such a thing as humane food production.

Food is deeply integrated into cultural artifacts, with tantalizing reminders of its abundance and variety on display in every corner of the man-made world. One can scarcely escape the sights and smells if one lives in society. A starving man would need to go deep into the wild if he wishes to escape the torment. Most urban trails that advertise food actually do lead to guaranteed food. And it isn't just the actual consumption that brings joy. Much of the pleasure lies in the anticipation. Man extends this pleasure with detours and details, while being secure in the knowledge that the meal is a given. So he teases himself with appetizers, he plays with flavors and spices, he gives it this treatment and that, he toys with the look and feel, he decorates his food. He combines meat and grain and plant matter and synthetics, all of which convert in his gut to the same blood glucose fuel. In the end, he must get a strong hit of sugar, or else all the play has been just a tease. To enjoy the maximal pleasure, he has also developed a mind-boggling array of exceedingly sugary foods, which bypass all the foreplay and get straight to the point in his body.

In much of the world today, man often eats to entertain himself, since true hunger rarely exists as a pleasure for him to break. No other animal entertains itself with food. This uniquely human characteristic results from the relative abundance of food and a rich tradition of various tastes and recipes specific to cultures. It is only under conditions of true hunger that one sees these associations stripped away. A shipwreck survivor won't bother making an elaborate sauce to go with the meat after a few weeks of not eating anything. At that point, all one craves is for the hunger pains to go away, along with the shakiness, the hallucinations and the cold. Thus, the satisfaction that a starving man derives from acquiring and consuming food is undeniably intense. Yet, the act of satiating oneself reduces the subsequent pleasure, with diminishing returns. Beyond a certain point, the situation flips, and ingesting more food results in physical discomfort.

If man regularly attempts to derive excessive pleasure from food, a tolerance builds up over time, allowing him to be able to consume ever larger amounts before reaching the point of inversion where the pleasure ceases and the discomfort begins. The process of stretching the gut and the mind's conception of adequate food happens over the years as plentiful food is chosen as a compelling means of daily entertainment, while abstaining from physical exertion. The end state of happiness after satiating oneself is no greater than before, but it takes a lot more food to get there. Various physical and chemical systems in the body now begin to creak under the burden of supporting all the excess flesh, giving rise to a new and chronic source of misery. Society's critical eye looks down harshly upon the obese man, further compounding his plight. This in turn drives him to seek refuge deeper in his familiar source of comfort, which is food.

Impoverished men suffer this fate more readily in the modern world. Given their limited spending power, they choose cheap, energy dense foods that last a long time, require minimal effort to prepare, and deliver the biggest rewards of sugar to the blood.

Furthermore, they lack the money or means to expend enough energy to offset their consumption. If one escapes obesity at all today, it is usually because of a strict adherence to a combination of dietary rules, eating habits, and regular physical exertion. These routines and restrictions are so deeply ingrained in modern man that by the time one is an adult, a complete absence of these behaviors would be a gross aberration. Even if one does not always succeed in following society's prescribed eating behavior, one is deeply aware of the expected behavior. In the daily drama that plays out between the mind and the appetite, tempting food is cast as the interfering and crafty villain, and the better tasting the food, the more evil it is. The very thing that sustains life is now also a daily source of guilt. Food is the channel for all of his anxieties about his health and appearance, about hurting animals, and about harming the planet.

No such paradox existed for early man. It was impossible for the primitive to overeat on a regular basis. The wild fruits and hard roots available to the primitive had much coarse roughage that had to be gotten through with tiresome chewing. Even with the advent of a cooking fire, these undeveloped plants did not yield their calories easily. Any fruits that got ripe enough to be sweet were immediately besieged by insects, birds, rodents and mammals. Aside from the occasional honey stolen from a bee hive, there was no source of pure sugar in the wild. Similarly, the flesh of animals hunted in the wild was lean and tough, which had a self-limiting effect on appetite. With the exception of mammalian brains, oils from fish, and rendered blubber from cold water creatures, fat was a rare and highly valued commodity. Finally, there were no refined carbohydrates to eat. Thus, an obese stone age man would have been both exceedingly rare and exceedingly fortunate. In contrast, man today can gorge himself daily on cake, candy, cookies and coke. All he has to do to get a big dose of sugar is get up, walk to his kitchen, and reach for the cereal or the fridge door.

THE ETERNAL SEARCH

Eating large amounts of rich food the first thing in the morning would be highly atypical for primitive man. Most foods don't store well in the wild, and get spoiled, infested or stolen within hours. Man didn't wake up to a breakfast buffet. In order to eat, he first had to forage and gather plants, or walk to a stream or lake to fish, or go on an expedition to set traps or hunt. Any acquired food would then be brought back to camp to be prepared over a communal fire. All of this took time and effort. Thus, the first few hours after daybreak were invariably spent on an empty stomach, and the prospect and timing of eating uncertain. It was only near sundown that he might return to camp and eat, if at all. This was not a matter of great concern to man, since that was the way it was.

The primitive likely had a significantly more relaxed relationship to food. This is despite him facing an occasional spell of starvation, compared to the perpetual abundance enjoyed by modern man. His knowledge and expertise from a lifetime of being immersed in hunting and gathering practices was so great that he could afford to express disregard for hunger. If the river was dry of fish today, there was always the forest with its riches, but one had to know where to look and how to find it. Anthropologists encountering the indigenous tribes of the Amazon found them so knowledgeable about their local wildlife that an individual could walk into the jungle alone and naked, and return days later with hand-crafted baskets full of plant and animal foods.

Of course, at times the primitive returned to camp empty-handed, but there was always another day to forage and hunt in nature. He simply lazed by the campfire, shrugged off the hunger, and entertained with bragging tales about the past instances of heroism in procuring food for the tribe. If things got really bleak, as they invariably did, no doubt he suffered, and watched others suffer or die too. In his conception, it was because the spirits were upset, and one just had to get the shaman to perform sacrificial rituals to appease them and all would be well again. Being witness to life and death on a daily basis, both of his own species and of the lives he took, the ancient hunter was under no illusions about what food meant. He saw things as they were, in the raw, naked and bloody. Some lives had to cease to exist so others could continue to exist. Yes, the primitive could be indifferent to hunger, but his food was always a blessing, a gift from the spirit world.

Modern man tries to affect indifference too, but his indifference is usually towards his food, not his hunger. He is simply not hungry often enough to learn to deal with it when the real thing strikes. He expresses this indifference in many ways. He may order up extravagant displays of rich food and then let it all go to waste. He thinks nothing of letting a butchered life form rot on the table while he talks and talks. He toys with his food and creates fanciful shapes as if it were mere putty for his amusement. He frequently eats while doubly engaged in what he considers more important activities. He relegates food to a mere necessity to sustain his activities, and views it as fuel to chow or gulp down. All this pretense of indifference falls flat rather quickly. Since he rarely if ever procures the food that he eats, he is always deeply insecure about its continued availability. The food in his belly is invariably store bought. It appeared out of nowhere, like magic, and now it is neatly arranged for him to enjoy. Lacking any real insight on how this daily miracle happens, he rightly fears that the magic may disappear at any moment, leaving him unprepared. Indeed, it only takes a short spell or the mere threat of food scarcity for his ancient fears about starvation to rise to the surface.

One reason man today rarely goes to a state of full hunger is because he feeds by the clock, whether his gut needs it or not. The clock and the periodic drumbeats of breakfast, lunch, and dinner are his primary cues to eat. Early in civilization, with the rise of grain agriculture and domestication of animals, the farming man had begun the practice of eating before he started his day. He needed to fill his stomach before going out to the field and expending large amounts of energy on working the land. Later on, feudal lords and factory owners demanded hard labor from their workers, and instituted short, set breaks for food and rest in between shifts. These practices might have been the origin of our rigid meal times, but they have since taken a life of their own. At least the farmer and the factory worker ate to sustain the hard labor they would perform. Man today does no such thing. His culture now reinforces these named windows of consumption, where one eats every few hours because one is supposed to. Being late for lunch or dinner implies that the generally agreed upon meal time has not been respected. Such deviations can cause friction among family, friends and acquaintances.

The grip of set mealtimes is so strong that even a solitary man keeps himself on a regular feeding cycle. There is nothing special about the clock hitting noon that should make him feel hungry for lunch, but if that's when he has been eating it in the preceding days, he is like the Pavlovian dog that has trained itself to salivate at the sound of a bell. He prefers to layer fresh food upon still undigested food because this avoids the inconvenience of having to consider whether one is hungry or not. Once the day has been broken up into these named eating segments, one can further subdivide the inbetween hours with entertaining tidbits called snacks, typically available in colorful packages with a variety of shapes, textures and flavors. Without these regular infusions of taste-based entertainment, the day lengthens unbearably. The hours become boring. If one is fasting out of choice, one begins to question that choice and one's previous resolution, like questioning the aesthetic judgement of an artist who chooses to paint a landscape totally devoid of color.

Sugar

Once there is sugar in the blood, there is some for the hungry brain too. It is no surprise then that food for the hungry man is so pleasurable. Brains are designed by evolution to release chemical rewards for behaviors that propagate a creature's life, such as ingesting food. The primitive had limited mechanisms available to him for triggering such rewards. He could feed hunger, he could get endorphin relief from some hurt, he could get warmth for the cold or vice versa, and he could enjoy the sensations of touch and sex. Sometime in prehistory though, he discovered other plant based substances that released the same reward chemicals in much greater amounts. Natural substances such as opium seeds, cannabis buds and coca leaves affect the brain in ways analogous to sugar. They reduce pain and satisfy cravings. In limited quantities, these substances are mostly harmless or even beneficial. The chemicals modulate his brain and allow him to experience breakthroughs that he might otherwise not achieve. Psychedelics such as Peyote cacti, Ayahuasca and Magic mushrooms bring man deep insight into the interconnectedness of all natural phenomena and his own perception.

Unfortunately for man, he then discovered how to manufacture highly purified and concentrated versions of these natural substances in industrial quantities. Ethanol, cocaine, opioids, methamphetamines, nicotine, and a thousand other substances are now part of his repertoire of chemical friends. Past the small beneficial dosages, these substances either just severely numb him, or uplift him effortlessly into euphoric highs. Unlike sugar intake, which was historically limited by the amount of food he could chew, he can ingest drugs in practically unlimited quantities. He can abuse these substances for the extreme highs that they provide, often to the detriment of his body. As the brain adapts to the new reality of constantly being swamped by a flood of its own chemical rewards, it stops producing them in quite the same amounts. This desensitization leads man to increase his dose, or else he suffers from the lows that are the inevitable flip side of the highs. He is now trapped in a cycle of his own creation, addicted to the substance. The miserable predicament of an addict is the only thing he has to show for his efforts at seeking happiness.

As with food addiction, being poor also makes man more susceptible to substance addictions. Drinking alcohol is a culturally acceptable means of forming an addiction and immersing oneself in it. Fermented fruit or grain, formed into wine or malt beer brews, have been available since the farming era. Prior to that, man and other primates had access to naturally produced alcohols such as that found in the ripe Marula fruit as it sits and rots on the ground. The percentage of alcohol in these crude precursors to spirits was very low, such that consumption was self limiting. The primitive did not have access to distillation equipment in the forest. Today, because the refinement and cultural integration of alcoholic drinks occurred alongside civilization, ethanol escapes comparison to other restricted drugs even though it is equally dangerous to an addict. The only thing that limits consumption for a thorough alcoholic is his paycheck and his ability to sit upright. In desolate places spread all across the world, the destruction is wrought plainly on working and non-working men alike, who drink until they empty their guts and their wallets, night after night, till they return home to hungry children and waiting wives.

The overall trend for modern man is of an ever diminishing connection to his food and whatever else he puts in his body. Convenience and efficiency have driven large numbers of people to shrink that relationship solely to the dimensions of flavor and satiation. There is an increasing lack of understanding of the origins of food, of the skills needed to prepare it, and of the meaning and fulfilment associated with food. Increasingly, man just sits his corpulent body down at the table of a round-the-clock, all-you-can-eat buffet of extinguished lives that he has neither hunted nor gathered, and which he then proceeds to ignore or let go to waste.

Can man restore a healthy relationship with food? A first step would be to examine whether he chooses sugar or other substances to compensate or substitute for a lack of fulfilment in his life. He can then try to replace those addictions with healthier alternatives. Then, he can make a small attempt to learn more about his food. Of course, he'll never approach the primitive's immense skills and knowledge of nature, and in any case the world isn't large enough anymore for him to return to ancient means of feeding himself. He cannot wilfully abandon eons of technological progress and pretend that the stone age still persists. Hunting and gathering if practiced in the modern world is just a light and entertaining diversion. If there is no game to be gotten, there is always the store. Man cannot turn back the clock and adopt a lifestyle for a world that doesn't exist any more. Instead, he can aim to appreciate the stunning ease with which has daily access to food. He can grow small quantities of his own plant foods, or even raise livestock. He can purchase whole foods in an unpackaged, unprocessed state, and break them down to prepare meals together with the family.

Next, he can attempt to break his constant feeding cycle by randomly forgoing meals. Occasional fasts remind him of the absolute blessing that is food. It resets his body and his brain to tolerate less sugar without entering into states of panic or alarm. It forces him to find other joys to pass the hours of the day than regular infusions of tasty food. This brings into focus the entertaining nature of modern food, and he can then differentiate between eating to relieve hunger versus mere boredom. It clears the air about his true condition, because in the fasted state, he can compare with total clarity of the mind his own situation to those unfortunate few who face starvation and fast involuntarily. He gains respect for what food truly is, which is the sacrificed lives of others.

In the final reckoning, the lack of food and hunger have immense capacity to inflict suffering in man. Yet, it is hard to derive anything more than baseline satisfaction from its availability. There is no extra pleasure to be derived from food in excess of needs. Attempts to derive endless pleasure from it only results in new forms of misery. One can definitely eat too much. There are consequences to overdoing it. Does this same pattern apply to other areas where man seeks happiness? Perhaps one can eat too much, but surely one cannot have too much money or stuff? These are the topics to consider next.

Stuff

*A woman was found dead in her own house four months
after she first disappeared. Police and canine units both
missed finding her body at their initial search of the
property because of the overwhelming chaos of clothing
and household items that she had hoarded, in stacks
running from floor to ceiling. Months later, her husband
eventually saw her shoes sticking out from under a pile
of stuff in a cluttered back room that he was cleaning
out. Crews on the scene had to cut through the drywall to
safely retrieve the body.*

- Recent news story

*Piling up material goods cannot fill the emptiness of
lives.*

- Jimmy Carter

Stuff. Belongings. Things. Man's possessions.

Of this he has many. The average man brings into his house and
keeps there a million manufactured goods of all kinds of materials
and constructions. He stuffs them in drawers and shelves, piles
them in corners, puts them in boxes, in his basement, in his
garage, in his car, and when he runs out of space he goes out
and rents more space to store his stuff. Why so much stuff? Does
more stuff make him happier? Why does he have more material
wishes than he can ever consume in one lifetime?

THE ETERNAL SEARCH

That man is possessed by his possessions is well known. His process of attachment to stuff is automatic and efficient. It begins the moment he eyes a new object as a potential owner, even before he actually owns it. Once he is tied to this object, any attempt to separate from it causes him distress in proportion to how much he values it, like that child that screams mine when his toy is taken away. The object owns a part of his identity now. He will thereafter be its caretaker and duly protect it from loss, harm or theft, until the object or the man himself ceases to exist. In the aftermath of plane crash landings, passengers have been seen reaching for their bags and jamming up the aisles, even as smoke fills the cabin. Tales abound of shipwreck victims who would not let go of their heavier-than-water valuables, such as gold, silver, and their money belts, which weighed them down and dragged them to the bottom of the ocean. Firefighters have been found charred to death in the aftermath of a fast moving forest fire, while still holding tight their chainsaws and other heavy equipment. Some were just a few hundred yards away from a shelter where they could have sprinted to safety, if only they could have been persuaded to just drop their tools and run.

Stuff demands space. After first bringing countless objects into his home and then finding himself surrounded by clutter, man is driven by a need to bring order to the mess. He often spends time organizing, categorizing and sorting through his stuff, to make things easy to find, to separate like from unlike, and to make sense of the chaos. He does not treat each object the same way though. A few attractive objects get more space and premium positioning, so they can shine alone and exposed. Other stuff, such as socks and supplies, get gathered up and hidden out of view, either because they are unsightly, or are too numerous to deal with. He first puts these things into boxes, some open to view, some closed, and then packs these into even larger boxes that he calls rooms. Houses are essentially the ever larger shells man needs for containing and protecting all of his stuff.

Stuff

What's all this stuff for? Perhaps a small handful of items found in a man's possession may be called original works of art or craft. These are objects that were created by the hand of an artist, either by the man himself or another man. In contrast, for primitive man, all of his possessions belonged in this category. The primitive's clothing, utensils, tools, weapons, instruments and medicaments all were typically self-crafted from raw materials. A useful object created out of the elements of nature takes on a special significance for the creator, one that is missing in modern mass manufactured goods. Most modern homes contain few or none at all of such truly original creations.

A few dozen or a hundred odd items found in a typical residence are truly essential for daily life. These could be food, cooking implements, utensils, tools, clothes, lights, heaters, plumbing fixtures, etcetera. Such utilitarian goods help man feed and take care of himself, his family and his surroundings. They protect him from the elements and provide him with physical and physiological comfort and safety. Transportation options and internet connected devices are also essential for living in the world today, as they enable his mobility and access to jobs, markets, society, friends and other places. Lack of essential goods can definitely impact quality of life. Thus, when man finally acquires a basic utility, his life satisfaction improves correspondingly.

What remains, that is, the vast majority of the numerous items that man keeps, are neither original works nor essential goods. Instead, these objects find space in his house because man assigns one or more of three traits to each of them. Firstly, man believes that an object may have some possible utility in the future, although this anticipated usefulness is a vague notion rather than anything certain. Secondly, man believes the object to be fashionable, that is, it is stylish, sophisticated, and possesses aesthetic value that improves him or his surroundings. Finally, man attaches sentimental value to the object, simply by virtue of it being associated with a shard of memory from his past or present life.

Truly utilitarian items cannot possibly number in the tens of thousands, despite man's belief in them. This is a case of his wants being far greater than his needs. Most houses contain fanciful multitudes and variants of objects far past what is strictly necessary. Sometimes he hoards objects because of memories of scarcity in the past. Even without that trauma, he simply can't let go of objects once acquired, because he is unable to rationalize the wastefulness of throwing away what he considers to be perfectly good. If he somehow ends up owning ten shovels in his tool shed, to him each one of them feels just as good and sturdy to hold as the other. While he is rationally aware of the slim likelihood that nine of them will break and thus justify the presence of the tenth one, his emotional attachment to each shovel is equally strong, and prevents him from getting rid of any at all. He hangs on to all ten of them.

The second trait of goods that attracts them to modern man is their fashion value. All fashions are mass manufactured statements regarding the style and currentness of the object to which they apply. Bombarded from all sides with a millions such pronouncements and claims, man accepts, imbibes and constantly updates his notion of what is fashionable without realizing it. Fashion applies to items such as clothing and shoes, of course, but increasingly, to any and all objects as varied as appliances, cars, pets, furniture, food, gadgets, and houses. A new fashion lures man as soon as the charm of the old fades, but the charm of the old fades so fast only because the new is constantly being pumped out by vast factories devoted to this task. Only the newest fashion is featured favorably and prominently in advertisements, at retail outlets, and as the personal belongings of those who influence others.

Function constrains stuff to look a certain way, and cultural norms further tighten the bounds on the appearance of objects. For instance, clothing must function to keep man protected, warm or cool as needed, and then society further expects that man clothe himself in ways appropriate to the setting. An outfit worn to the beach must not only act like beachwear in terms of being able to deal with water, sun, sand and salt, but it must look like beachwear too. A stiff woolen suit would not fit the occasion nor be functional, just as the bikini would be doubly out of place at a cold fall funeral. Similarly, cars must drive like cars and do a variety of things that cars do. This forces them to conform to the standard design of a domed see-through cabin over a chassis with four rubber tires. A sports car must be further constrained in terms of proportions and streamlining if it is to convey itself instantaneously as sporty. Houses must serve the homeowner's needs, be built to code, and be equipped with standard fixtures and certified equipment. Beyond that though, a house must also be instantaneously familiar and welcoming, to the host and guests alike. Doors can have their hinges placed on the left or right sides, but never on the top or the bottom. No burglar breaking into a home ever encounters a scene so disorientingly unfamiliar that he abandons the break-in.

To the extent that functional things can vary in form though, lies the huge potential for fashion to influence purchases. Man has a finely developed eye for minute variations in shades and shapes. Primitive man used his discerning eye to interpret the signs of nature, such as insect, bird and animal dynamics, weather, rock and soil patterns, floral and fruiting patterns, etcetera. If the primitive wanted to know which stone to use as flint and which would make a good spearhead, which gourd to crack open when ripe and which to use as a water bottle, which root to dig up in the desert when thirsty and where to find it, which anthill to stake out and when to catch the plump and juicy fat winged males as they appear, then he needed to pay attention to shapes, colors and shades.

THE ETERNAL SEARCH

With fashion, man copied nature's color palette and then surpassed it. Stuff comes in infinite variety, carefully curated and grouped in accordance with the latest trends. They impart man with glitz and glamour, but it's more than that. His things help to craft an exclusive image for him. The clothes he wears, the car he drives, the bag he carries, all are carefully to craft a unique look, but this look cannot be too unique. It cannot deviate so far from norms that it comes across as bizarre or uncategorizable. It must convey an instantly recognizable image, as conceived by those who created and propagated that fashion. A man identifying himself as a sophisticated, confident and rugged man's man, one who appreciates the finer things but is not afraid to get his hands dirty, may want to fill his wardrobe with an image appropriate selection of classic button-down shirts with roll-up sleeves, hard wearing twill jeans, and full-grain leather shoes and belts. Of course, he can never go wrong with a cashmere sweater in his closet. The ladies appreciate a well-groomed man, so he may also want to invest in some quality hair products and aftershave. And it goes without saying, every man should own a well made two-button suit as his armor for everyday use, a serious dark double-breasted affair for when he wants to dress up and bring a hint of swagger to those formal dinner evenings, and finally, a light summery jacket for those casual occasions when life can throw anything at him. Fashion advertising creates a thousand anxieties in man, and then whispers a million options into his ear for easing them.

High fashion stuff, especially conspicuously extravagant stuff such as expensive art, jewelry, cars, etcetera, signals excess wealth. The excess wealth in turn indicates an ability to easily support a mate or a family. This makes spectacularly extravagant yet useless stuff particularly attractive to both to the suitor who flaunts these possessions, and to the mate he seeks to attract. This is an ancient form of sexual signalling, similar to the peacock's feathers. A primitive who spent much time in carving ornate patterns onto his spears may have signalled to his mate that he was such a capable hunter that providing food for the family would be a trifling matter to him. While this trait may have had some evolutionary benefit in the past, when life was more precarious, the contribution of stuff towards sustaining a modern family is mostly flat beyond a certain point. Most members of modern society are far past the threshold that their possessions are what help them survive or survive better. Still, the lure of stuff as a signal for reproductive potential is strong, which is precisely why sexual symbols are in turn effectively used to sell stuff.

The last trait that man assigns to his possessions is sentimental value. This category can be very broad, as it encompasses nearly all aspects of one's personal history. Items from one's childhood, items that once belonged to a friend or relative or ancestor, items dearly won or nearly lost, items found or stolen, items built or repaired by oneself, items acquired during travel and vacation, items used to celebrate or mourn, items that mark highs or lows, items from past relationships, items from past interests, items recalling past life phases, items denoting membership to groups or lifestyles, items that recall tough times, trauma or distress, items quirky or quaint or meaningless, items that convey one's status, titles, sophistication, knowledge, virtue, hard work, experience or accomplishments, and lastly, items whose sentimental value arises from being delightful discovered again one day, many years after their existence in the house had been forgotten altogether.

Do all his things make man happy? As they say, things fall apart. Thus, the ability of an object to bring happiness is offset by its latent and ever-present potential to cause misery from its loss. Any satisfaction he gains from the ongoing value of objects is subject to certain amounts of adaptation. Meanwhile, the eventual and inevitable loss of the object's worth always hangs by a thread. The worrying that he endures as caretaker for every object in his possession negates nearly all the happiness that the object might provide. This is the primary reason why his joy from acquiring new stuff fades fast and is replaced with the caretaker's anxiety.

Man's worrying gaze does not linger on his possessions uniformly. The more valuable the item is to him, or the more fanciful its looks or construction, the more he worries about its wellbeing. Indeed, when a shiny and much valued object finally smashes to pieces or gets stolen, this can bring surprising relief to him once the initial distress fades, for he knows that now he can finally stop worrying about that dreaded event happening. It is better for such a valuable object to be completely and irreversibly destroyed, than to be mildly dented or rendered partially non-functional. He fares better psychologically when there is no chance at all of the object returning to its past unblemished glory.

Over the course of his life, man pours a significant fraction of his time, money and energy into acquiring, transporting, storing, maintaining, protecting and caretaking his stuff. Naturally, he feels an obligation to enjoy his possessions, otherwise all his effort would be for nothing. A direct consequence of stuff ownership then is that he often spends more time touching and interacting with his stuff than with the people around him. If he spends a lot of time indoors, it is a direct consequence of the fact that that's where all his stuff lives too. Seen in this light, a house is simply a device for passive indoor storage of a dormant human being and his lifeless companions.

In contrast, primitive man spent far a greater proportion of his time outdoors. He lacked indoor lighting and plumbing, big houses with lots of secluded rooms, and the myriad gadgets and entertainment options that enable man today to spend hours

Stuff

inside in complete isolation. Perhaps the primitive sat near a communal fire as he worked on his tools or crafts, where he could still converse with his fellow human. Today, man is often silent and alone as he stays indoors, with no regular companion by his side. He hibernates even in summer, and hides from the warmth of the sun on cold days. The more stuff he owns, indeed the more he may suffer from feelings of isolation and loneliness.

In terms of sheer numbers, the vast majority of the stuff purchased today, and immediately trashed, are disposable items. These are all the single-use cups, cans, bottles, bags, diapers and packaging of course, but increasingly, also items such as electronics, clothing and medical equipment. Disposable goods are a convenient solution to both the space problem and the caretaking problem. When stuff is disposable, man is relieved of the burden of having to find a place in his home for the item, because it will be consigned to the garbage can as soon as he is done. He is freed from the obligation to repair, maintain and protect the item past a single use. Constructed out of cheap materials and priced accordingly low, disposable items allow for an easier decision to buy. They stand out to him as a better alternative to making a commitment with a pricier item. If he gets a dud item that doesn't work as advertised, he paid so little for it that he can simply shrug his shoulders, toss it into the trash, and move on.

Increasingly, massive quantities of man's possessions reside in virtual worlds. These could be his songs, words, pictures, moving pictures, games, conversations, interactions, social histories, financial transactions, work documents, records, etcetera. Just like he does with real objects, and for pretty much the same reasons, he hoards and collects virtual items at an astonishing rate. These items exist on an atomic scale and are thus vanishingly small in terms of the space they take up in the world. Man however cannot pack his consideration of things on an atomic scale. To him, a virtual object feels just as real as something he can touch and handle, and is no less compact in terms of the neurons it occupies in his brain. In the confines of his skull, these items catch his attention the same way as real objects do.

Given its compactness, the sheer quantity of virtual stuff that man can accumulate can be staggeringly immense, and so thus can grow his burden as caretaker. He has the same need to organize, arrange and protect these items, and spend time with them. He feels distressed when this stuff goes missing or stolen. In addition, for each item whose existence he is aware of in his personal collection, a much larger number exist outside of his awareness, hidden from his sight but yet associated with his name. These virtual goods are owned by various large corporations, and used to document him, to understand his tastes, and to entice and influence him when the need arises. Being vaguely aware of this, man has yet another source of anxiety to deal with. No matter what he is doing, he is constantly on the watch for being robbed of his virtual goods, and worries about how they will be used to mislead him in the future.

Virtual possessions define man's identity in the virtual world, and he is attached to them just like he is to shiny things in the real world. Once he has crafted an image for himself, he is slave to his own creation. If that virtual image withers or dies, a little bit of him dies with it. Knowing this, corporations that store the constituents of his image on their platforms reel him into a never-ending cycle of forced interactions. His identify requires frequent maintenance in the form of his latest opinions, pictures, status updates and posts in order to look fresh and sophisticated. His family and friends come to know his virtual image more intimately than the flesh and blood version, and he dare not let it go stale. Once again, the stuff that he owns ends up owning him. Man's possessions once formed the currency for a rich and dynamic cycle of gifting. All primitive societies placed great significance on festivals and feasting with members of the tribe and of neighboring tribes. A key element of these gatherings was a ritual exchange of gifts. While trading for necessary goods might have been one driver of these exchanges, often the motive was to strengthen relationships. Ethnologists have described intricate and carefully ordained give and take of all manner of goods such as food, gemstones, shells, wine, tobacco, weapons, masks, figurines, garments, etcetera. This trade was conducted by the elders as accompaniments to cementing an alliance, giving away a bride, paying thanks to the spirits, celebrating a harvest, or for no other reason at all besides the excitement of gifting. The primitive thus viewed his possessions not just in terms of their intrinsic value, but also their potential for building relationships. The more one gave, the more one gained in terms of stronger interpersonal networks. Contrast this with man today, whose countless things sit collecting dust uselessly and doing little to promote his cause in society.

Shiny objects are unparalleled in their ability to inspire envy and feelings of inadequacy in man. Other men sell him goods based on this principle, by dangling a dazzling variety of items in his field of vision wherever he turns. He attempts to reduce his anxiety, primarily by purchasing a copy of the coveted object for himself. If this is not possible, he may resort to other means, such as destroying or stealing the object, lashing out in anger, distracting himself, or getting depressed. If he can just buy it though, he eventually will. He buys not out of necessity, of course, but to improve his esteem, relieve his anxiety, and feel some excitement. There is a pleasurable buzz felt in the moments shortly before and after the purchase. In seeking out this thrill, he will engage in any number of irrational and impulsive buys that may later disappoint him. He repeatedly fails to consider his future regret while making the purchases.

THE ETERNAL SEARCH

Cultural norms encourage man in his stuff addiction. In many settings, it is rude to present oneself in a manner that suggests that one has not spent as much as one could have. The unspoken directive does not explicitly state that man must buy more stuff, but when translated into practical terms, that is what it ends up being. One does not present a guest with old cutlery or seat them on beaten up furniture. One must not display inferior goods at a social gathering, to avoid being seen as miserly or unsophisticated. One must dress well to command respect, and since clothes go out of style, this implies buying into new fashions. Other men are in the business of selling, and continually develop and propagate new norms to drive purchase behavior. A variety of holidays, festivals and commemorative events all now require reciprocal gift giving. With the rest of society serving as a baseline for how to behave, one must be careful not to appear as cheap. If one can afford it, one must. Man being a highly social animal, he takes that message to heart, even at his personal misery. He buys into the belief that surrounding himself with the finest objects is his ticket to being accepted into all of society.

The cumulative effect of all this personal and societal compulsion for consumption is financial stress. Man endures disputes with family and friends about money. He spends long hours at work, earning to pay for what he wants to buy, or more typically, for what he has already bought. He constantly feels trapped under the burden of bills and expenses. He hates his job or his commute, but is unable to pursue more satisfying options or endeavors for fear of falling into debt and losing everything. Even if he is wealthy and can afford to spend, his stuff addiction harms society. Money that could have been spent towards improving quality of life is instead locked up in goods that sit collecting dust and crumbling to dust inside homes and garages. Natural resources are destroyed, the earth is polluted, and countless plant, animal and human lives suffer and die

Stuff

from the environmental impacts of industrial production. By grabbing land and resources for mass factories, man takes away the means for other species to survive. The global consumption of stuff is the single biggest force changing the planet's surface.

What can one say in summary about the sea of stuff that man swims in? He needs some essential goods to stay out of misery, of course. Beyond that, despite the protests of every shopper who is currently experiencing the thrill of a purchase, stuff does nothing to enhance man's happiness beyond a temporary thrill. Once he has acquired the object, its charm fades fast, and the caretaker's burden sets in. He must now acquire the next shinier object in order to feel good again. Adherence to cultural norms and a desire for acceptance drive man to purchase much more stuff than would be necessary if he lived in isolation. Eventually, he finds himself seated alone on top of a pile of goods the size of a small mountain. In owning these goods, they come to own him. They demand his time and his attention, and they isolate him. He is now the material man, living alone on his mountain of goods.

That everyone else also accumulates stuff obsessively does not make any one man's behavior rational. His out-of-control addiction to material goods is objectively an insanity, irrespective of what others around him do. If all men are fundamentally flawed, then bizarre behaviors can be indeed be present in all. This does not change the facts for each individual who is caught in the cycle of consumption. The widespread nature of consumption does make it difficult for him to exit the cycle. When thoroughly inundated by stuff, a rejection of materialism stands out as a conscious statement of an alternate lifestyle, and requires great effort to carry out. This rejection can also be carried to an extreme. If he spends too much time and effort in attempting to obsessively clean out the clutter in his life, he has achieved nothing at all even when he succeeds. A minimalist

32

can obsess about stuff too, just in a different way. His obsession is with reducing the count. Reducing one's possessions to an arbitrary ideal is not desirable if doing so gets in the way of his interactions with fellow men.

Instead, what man needs is the strength to form his own opinions regarding the necessity of goods. He can develop a mindful awareness of when he seeks to acquire stuff just to make himself feel better for a fleeting few moments. The trick for man is to recognize the extent to which goods enable him to be a healthy individual, to take care of himself and his family, to participate in healthy interactions with his fellow man and society, and reject all other items as superfluous. When he does this, he becomes indifferent to the false enticements of goods that claim to change his life for the better. He cares about stuff only to the extent that they truly improve his well-being in a lasting way. He can make space in his home and his mind for other things but things. He can then look past the mountains of his dead stuff and see the river of life flowing just beyond.

Money

The best thing about money is that it gives you the freedom to choose your own form of misery.

- Groucho Marx

Money, so they say,
Is the root of all evil today.
But if you ask for a rise,
It's no surprise,
That they're giving,
None away.

- Money, by Pink Floyd

Every man has heard something along the following lines. Money won't make you happy. Money is evil. It can't buy you love. It'll drive your true friends away, and leave you lonely. Don't spend your life chasing after it. You can't take it to the grave anyways. In various forms, these and similar sentiments are so commonly expressed in society that one would scarcely question the basic nugget of truth. Yet, what David Gilmour was singing amidst the chaotic drumbeats and jangly guitars is the more complete picture. Yes, money may be evil and will not make man happy, but everybody still wants it. How come? More money, more, more, more. What's going on?

THE ETERNAL SEARCH

It is illustrative to first examine the origins of money to determine its potential for happiness. A common belief is that money originated to facilitate easier trade of goods. This argument holds that the birth of all symbolic money, whether coins, trinkets or paper money, had an economic driver. Currencies developed as merchants sought more efficient means of exchanging goods than barter. Certainly, using money is a lot easier than trying to exchange twenty sacks of potatoes for one and a half cows. Once money came into being, all a trader needed to do was carry a few small pieces of metal stamped with the king's seal. The royal image acted as a guarantee that even a stranger who accepted these coins as payment was getting something of genuine worth. Something that could be further traded for real goods, as long as all of the king's subjects had continued trust in that currency.

The problem with the economic theory of money's origin though is that it may be getting the order of things wrong. It presupposes that the large scale trade made possible by money itself gave rise to money. Instead, did money perhaps originate earlier for other reasons, and the trade that relied on that money develop later? Evidence suggests that may indeed be the case. In its earliest use, money was a marker of personal obligations. If a man owed someone money, if he was in debt, then he or his family members were undoubtedly indentured, even enslaved, until he had repaid his obligations. If he didn't have the coins on him, then he would have to put in hard labor with his muscles until he had produced an equivalent amount of goods. Who would or could impose such a demonic debt?

In the egalitarian society typical of hunter gatherer tribes, no one man had sufficient clout or the need to accumulate an immense wealth of goods, to lend it, and to later demand repayments. Sure, there may have been a leader, but his grass hut and its contents looked scarcely any different from the huts of others. For the prehistoric nomad, goods were of a perishable nature, like meats or fruit, or difficult or impractical to carry around in more numbers than one needed, like bows and spears. Furthermore, other members of the tribe were quite capable of acquiring or crafting those same goods with their own skills. The unspoken agreement was of a daily give and take, of dynamic cooperation. If one returned empty handed from a hunting or fishing expedition, others had to share their catch with him, provided he had done the same for them in the past. If one did not reciprocate, one risked being exiled from the tribe. In most cases, being exiled and trying to survive all alone was difficult, resulting in suffering or even death. Therefore, everyone reciprocated, but beyond that, nobody owed anything significant to anybody. Any deep obligation that the primitive felt was reserved for the spirit world that provided him with life-giving natural resources. His debt was to the Gods alone.

Then came the invention of agriculture. Farming is the practice of growing as much food as possible when the conditions are right, and then storing the harvest to get through the lean times. When one is preparing the land, planting seeds, or tending to the crop, he is not hunting or gathering for daily needs. Farming is thus a specialization that forces dependence on others. This arrangement favors ever larger settlements, which further increases the pressure on the land and the farmer to produce, since the hunting and gathering can no longer satisfy demand. These large settlements produce large amounts of food, which often represent an entire year's worth of labor to the community. To lose the crop would be ruinous to the settlement. The need arises for armed warriors to protect the settlement and their stored harvest from neighboring marauders. Even in times of peace, they need hierarchies to impose equitable division of labor and lay down the law. Someone needs to sit and govern at the top of this hierarchy. Someone also needs to commune with the spirits, to obtain blessings for the entire populace, and to be a surrogate God. A role is thus created for a protector, a pope, a chieftain, a feudal lord, a king, an overlord.

THE ETERNAL SEARCH

At the outset of agrarian societies, a farming household had no need to engage in trade. Its needs were met adequately by small scale barter and give-and-take with neighboring households. Yet, they still had to pay homage to their overlord. When the crops were bountiful, the chief of a small settlement might have received a portion of the extra produce as a tribute. However, this gets cumbersome quickly as the settlement gets larger and the number of people giving tribute grows proportionally. Instead of having sacks and sacks of perishable food be brought to his house, the overlord might just want to keep track of the farmer's seasonal obligation on small clay tablets or bits of stamped metal. Markers of debt were created. These pieces of debt, once established, then begin to circulate among the populace as they traded personal obligations. This then became money.

As even a casual gardener knows, some years the harvest will fail completely. Seasons are fickle, rainfall is unpredictable, and pests or diseases can decimate crops. The farming household is indentured by their contracts to their overlords. In addition to starving, the family is now in debt. They can no longer erase the obligations marked clearly in the clay tablets at the overlord's house with sacks of grain. Instead, they have no choice but to offer the last thing they possess, which is the excess energy contained in their already lean bodies. The overlord takes this energy in the form of free labor, and in exchange gives the hungry family just enough food to survive. An indentured laborer must endure many insults, but the one that hurts the most is the loss of free will as he toils to repay what he owes, or face certain starvation. This was the origin of slavery. Debt is thus the same as money.

Across cultures, man displays a dislike for being obligated to anyone, and his choice of words reflect this. He says thank you when someone does him a favor. Thank is really an archaic English form of the future tense of think. What he is really saying when he thanks someone then is that he will think of them in the future when it is his turn to reciprocate. Saying thanks is thus simply the verbal equivalent of giving someone a metal coin to clear the obligation. The German danke has similar origins to thanks, as a future form of denken or think. In Portuguese, obrigado conveys the same message, that one acknowledges that one is obligated in the future, and this reminder of the reciprocal nature of favors wipes the slate clean of obligations. The French merci originates from a Latin word for wages, fees or price. Again, one is saying thanks to substitute for a concrete obligation. In Sanskrit and Hindi, dhanyavad similarly ties the act of giving thanks to dhanya or wealth. Many other languages use words of similar construct to allow man to steer clear of a pending obligation in the future.

A true mark of a civilized society is when it abolishes slavery and establishes safeguards against it. Yet, slavery still exists in parts of the world. Women and children are still sold into slavery, either for sex or unpaid labor. Untold numbers of small farmers in impoverished nations still fall prey to unscrupulous money lenders, and entire families commit suicide when they are unable to repay their debts. For the rest of humanity though, these are fortunate times to be alive. There are of course modern forms of debt, but these are strictly financial obligations to banks, credit card companies, mortgage companies, and businesses. If one is a law abiding citizen in a relatively wealthy part of the world, he may lose his house and his car and everything else he owns to debt and bankruptcy, but he won't ever lose his freedom. Unless he willingly steals or commits fraud, chances are he can avoid getting thrown into jail and enduring forced labor.

This is a marked change from how things used to be early in civilization, when being penniless was one and the same as being a slave. Given these sobering origins of money, it is no surprise that man is driven to accumulate it beyond reason. Culture retains the memory of painful stories from times gone by. Man remembers that in the not too distant past, owing money implied unfulfilled obligations that ultimately led to a life in shackles. If he got too deep in debt, he or his family might have been taken away. Money was the original get-out-of-jail card. Even though slavery has become rare in modern times, he still fears the prospect of a complete loss of soveriegnty and free will. He obsessively collects those pieces of debt markers, because, who knows, he might need them one day to trade himself out of an impending loss of freedom.

The question remains, whether money increases happiness. No doubt, in societies where freedom is not a guaranteed right, money serves as a security blanket against slavery. At this level of existence, having no money means one might have no choice but to go into bonded labor to survive. Money then directly allows man to retain his free will and sovereignty. Even in free societies, if the financial circumstances are dire, money definitely raises his happiness. If he suffers daily from hunger, cold and deprivation, or lack access to basic shelter, sanitation and medical care, then his fundamental human needs are not being met. Although it is still possible to be happy even in these stark conditions, the daily insults to his well-being are not easy to ignore. Any injection of wealth usually tends to result in a direct and immediate improvement in this situation, and thus positively impacts life.

Then there are those numerous folks who cannot claim to be in abject poverty, yet live from paycheck to paycheck. A lack of disposable cash stings them daily, and without any savings, they are always one mistake or misfortune away from disaster. They might not suffer from hunger or lack basic amenities, but they do not have any slack in their finances. Their lives are a constant juggling and balancing act, of trying as best as they can to patch the holes by borrowing from one place to pay the other. They need to pay for dental work, but they don't have insurance, so they take out a cash advance, but then their car breaks down, and they need that car to get to work so they can get that paycheck at the end of the month to clear the cash advance, so now they overdraw their bank account to fix that, so now the bank charges overdraft fees on top of everything, and so on and so forth. The constant stress of such a life makes money a sweet and welcome reward.

Once man gets past this stage of rocky finances though, things get tricky. Beyond a certain income level that is adequate to ensure a stable lifestyle, any additional inflow of money does little towards putting a constant smile on his face. More money most likely won't increase his self-reported life satisfaction scores. The fact is, rich people, no matter how insanely rich, might just be no more happier than the moderately wealthy. Most men might nod their heads in general agreement at hearing this, but their own actions betray an endless pursuit of riches. It is as if they believe their specific situation is uniquely different from that of all others, and their happiness will indeed be boosted by more wealth. Why is this?

Clearly, there are some flaws in man's reasoning. Fundamentally, he is completely unable to predict his own happiness as a function of having more money. In addition, he fails to predict other men's happiness as a function of them having more money. Both forms of flawed thinking are equally important in contributing towards his misunderstanding of money's effects. Yet, the first one surprises him more, because he expects to know himself better than anyone else. If other people can't be happy despite having millions in the bank, he can easily dismiss this by saying that it must be their own fault. When the same thing happens to him though, he is dumbfounded. He is unable to accurately predict his own state of mind.

THE ETERNAL SEARCH

When man thinks that if only he had lots of money, he would be happier, what he is forgetting is that once he has that money, that's not how he'll be thinking. Big lottery winners are happy for a few months after their large monetary gain, yet in a year's time they are no happier than they were in the past. Desires simply rise along with the influx of money. After a while one gets used to the extra cash. Now he has new expectations, and the gap between those new expectations and his reality form the basis for his happiness or unhappiness. He gets accustomed to eating in fancier restaurants, living in fancier houses, and taking fancier vacations to the point that none of these seem fancy any more. The result is no net permanent increase in his happiness level, no matter how wealthy he gets. Psychologists call this constant process of adapting and reverting to a baseline level of happiness as being on the hedonic treadmill.

Hedonic adaptation applies both to positive and negative events. However, it is far easier to adapt to positive events than negative ones. If someone loses a limb, he may still return to his old happiness level after a few years of adaptation, yet he may retain a lingering nostalgia about some cherished aspect of his past, like being able to play football. Nostalgia explains why events such as divorce, death of a spouse, unemployment, and disability cast a long shadow across time, and tend to linger in the minds long past the event. This suggests that a key element of the adaptation process is how easy it is to remember or forget a past state. If someone gets demoted and has to take a drastic pay cut at work, his insensitive colleagues may unwittingly yet constantly remind him of his loss by talking about all the nice vacations they take that he can no longer afford. This will rub salt in his wounds until finds another job where his co-workers are in a similar income league. He quits so he can forget the insult that he can't adapt to.

Money

Now imagine what happens when someone wins the lottery. At first he might not know what to do with all the extra money. Chances are though that over time, the activities he partakes in and the people he hangs out with will move up the wealth ladder. One tends to mostly associate with others from a similar income bracket. It is unlikely that he has a lot of friends who are significantly poorer or richer than him. In first place, he is less likely to meet such potential friends. Social circles are heavily filtered into buckets sorted by wealth levels. The school he went to, the neighborhood he lives in, the clubs he hangs out in, the friends his friends have, all get stratified this way. Furthermore, even if he does have the chance to be friends with someone from a very different income strata, the potential for awkward moments during straightforward social interactions is high. Imagine being constantly challenged by the simple task of picking a suitable restaurant. Naturally, he then tends to fall out of touch with the set of folks he used to hang out with. Any reminders of his past state are usually out of sight, out of mind. Hedonic adaptation sets in, and he doesn't even remember what it was like to cut coupons and shop in thrift stores anymore.

Here then arises the issue of absolute wealth versus relative wealth. Maybe common wisdom about money is wrong because it draws on studies of absolute wealth. Demographic surveys over the years indeed show constant happiness levels while nations as a whole get richer. Chances are that compared to his parents' or grandparents' generation, someone alive today has a bigger house and car, enjoys a greater abundance and variety of food, has better healthcare, takes more exotic vacations, and has access to fancy technology at the fingertips. Yet he reports the same life satisfaction as his grandpa did. Could this be because everyone else around him is richer as well, so he doesn't feel rich? No matter how hard he spends and consumes his way to happiness, it doesn't work. If other folks can do the same, at best he can just keep up with his peers, and that's no fun.

Relative wealth perhaps matters more to him because his brain is a comparison machine that finds it hard to ignore disparities. Being surrounded by richer folks doesn't sit right with him. He would feel much better to possess mediocre wealth in a nation full of poor folks. He can then claim a higher status from his unique and blessed financial position relative to the others.

Complicating this picture though, and counteracting the life satisfaction increase from higher relative wealth, is the entitlement effect. Entitlement refers to the belief that one's superiority, higher status and importance should result in getting special treatment or consideration. The jerk in the fancy sports car who doesn't stop for pedestrians at the crosswalk, the rich lady cutting ahead of others at the airport queues because she and only she is running late, the trust fund kid who thinks that he can get away with rape because he's never not gotten what he's wanted before, or the politician who bends the laws of a nation and steals money from the poor, all suffer from a pronounced entitlement effect. When the consequences from such behavior catch up with them, they are genuinely surprised, hurt, and feel as if they are being singled out. Nobody is immune to how entitlement affects thinking. Rich people get used to having their way wherever money can grease the wheels and ease the pains. However, when they encounter situations where waving wads of cash at the problem doesn't make it go away, their sense of entitlement leads to frustration, outrage, denial, and anger. Various aspects of life can trigger this dissatisfaction, but the obvious ones are the rules and constraints of life, whether natural or man-made. Death, disease, taxes and laws are typical examples.

On balance then, the higher status from relative wealth still only contributes a tiny sliver to the overall picture of satisfaction. Why more money beyond a point brings no permanent happiness has to do with man's moment to moment experience of life as a biological entity, as a flesh and blood animal just like all the other living and breathing creatures. This experience is based on two things and two things alone. How the mind feels, and how the body feels, forming a real-time mental and physical health scorecard. The money he has is a narrow and abstract concept, an ethereal and ghostly thing that has little influence to exert over these scores.

The mental score is made up of things he may be feeling at any instant, such as frustration, boredom, depression, hopelessness, loneliness, and grief on the negative side, and excitement, engagement, connectedness, cheerfulness, hopefulness, and elation on the positive side. The richness of life and it's varied accompanying emotions make it impossible to boil down the moment to moment feeling to any single driver. Money can buy man some tickets here and there, but there's no guarantee that he will enjoy the ride. As Groucho Marx's quote that opens this chapter illustrates, in essence all money does is help to change the setting, where man can then feel exactly the same as he always did.

The physical scorecard is even less likely to be influenced by money. The body constantly sends moment to moment reports of its state. Whether he likes it or not, man endlessly hears messages such as I'm hungry, I'm sleepy, I'm tired, and my back hurts. Or worse, he hears things such as I'm delirious and vomiting from dengue fever, or I'm in severe pain and drowning in blood from a bullet in my lungs. Occasionally, he gets upbeat messages, such as from the taste of delicious food, the rush from smoking a cigarette, or the sensory pleasures of an orgasm. Many of these positive body reports are actually the relief felt from a pent up desire being satisfied, and once sated, the fleeting pleasures dissipate. Adaptation kicks as well. If caviar, cognac or cocaine is a daily event, then it isn't special anymore, and the only time he really notices is when it isn't available. No matter his wealth then, man's physical score can at best approach the alright level and hang on. There is no cap on the suffering he can and will endure, and the variety of forms in which suffering is available are truly astounding. Ultimately, disease and distress do not spare the rich either.

Clearly then, man fails to accurately predict the effect of money on his satisfaction with his life. Now consider the second kind of flaw in his reasoning, when he tries yet fails in envisioning what might make others happy. Imagine a busy executive taking a quick lunch break from his office. He has no time for a relaxed meal, so he just walks outside his building, sits on a bench, and continues to work. As he sends messages on his phone, he absently chews on a leftover bagel that he had picked up earlier with his morning coffee. The bagel is stale and he isn't really hungry, but he eats anyways, because he is facing a long afternoon ahead. That dry bagel brings him little joy. He's even slightly annoyed to have to eat it. Meanwhile, across the street from the executive, a vagrant stands watching. He is starving, having eaten little to nothing in three days. He tries not to stare, but that bagel in the executive's hand is making his mouth water. He can smell it, he can hear the chewing, and he can almost taste it. The vagrant simply cannot imagine how the bagel wouldn't be a source of happiness to anyone.

When he desires it yet lacks it, money inspires envy in man like few other things. If someone else is blessed with good looks or athleticism, he can shrug his shoulders and say it wasn't in his genes. Traits like erudition, reputation, and expertise can be acquired, but only over time. On the other hand, a big load of cash, and hearsay stories of how someone else got their hands on such a load, tantalize him with an equal opportunity tag that claims that anyone can have it with just the right mix of luck, skill, and effort. There is no rule that says that one can only acquire this much money and only this fast. Monetary gains can be practically limitless, and so can his desire for it also be limitless. He believes that all he needs to do is keep trying and keep wanting, and it will come. The reality is something else, as anyone who has tried to run a business especially knows. Yet, the eagerness with which society and media promote the stories of the notably wealthy ensures that envy remains strong and chronic.

Money is incredibly addictive. Man is irrationally attracted to money, to the point that he at times values it more than a similar or larger value of goods that can be easily traded for even more cash. Of course, money helps him survive in modern civilization, but the test of addiction is when his desire for it far exceeds what is needed to get by, and when he pursues it at the expense of his own health and wellbeing. If the motive for being employed at work was simply to earn what is needed to ensure survival, the average man would work far less than he typically does. Consider a hypothetical contract, one that allows someone to purchase a lifetime guarantee of basic necessities. In return for a one-time payment now, he will be guaranteed food, water and shelter for as long as he is alive. This is essentially an insurance policy on survival. If money was primarily about survival, such contracts would be fairly common and popular. They don't exist, primarily because there is no demand for it. Anyone who has the money to afford such a contract tends to value hanging on to it a lot more even than a guaranteed supply of survival necessities.

Lottery winners think in similar fashion. When the lottery board presents the winner with the option to take a multi-million dollar payout now, or receive annual payments of a few hundred thousand dollars each spread out over a few decades, their response is predictable. Most folks will take the lump sum payment. This is true even if the present value of the annual payouts is much larger than the heavily taxed lump sum payout.

Does the lottery winner perhaps feel more secure by getting all the money in their own hands as soon as possible? Intuitively, people realize that they cannot be trusted with such a large sum of money not to blow through it. It's not about security at all. It's about the addiction, and the addict wants as high of a high as possible, right now, not later.

In an effort to gain more wealth, man will sacrifice other realms of life that are more important to his overall happiness. For instance, he may work so much that he has no time left to enjoy his days, which he notices and complains about, of course. Yet, he does not want to go back to earning a little bit less in order to have more time. Paradoxically, he fights even harder for the right to work more and potentially earn more. Essentially, he hopes to earn his way out of trouble. He takes on stressful jobs with long commutes. He has no time for himself or for others. He forgets to stop and smell the flowers and to smile at strangers. He loses patience alike for the young and rambunctious, and the old and slow. He forsakes any time-consuming interests outside of work. He neglects friends and family to the detriment of those relationships. He even neglects his own health. All of these sacrifices impact him in terms of poor life satisfaction.

All of this is presuming that man stays on the right side of the law and relies on hard work alone to earn his money. Of course, many will fall prey to temptation and resort to unethical or illegal means. The temptation of money is so great that for every sphere of life that has a legal, above the board version, there is someone who is risking his personal safety or freedom to operate a parallel, under the table version. A bottomless pit of opportunity exists for the unethical man, where fraud, thievery, robbery, corruption and extortion are just the obvious and old fashioned ways of operating. For the sophisticated hustler, the new digital age offers a million semi-legal or completely illegal ways of making it rich.

Money

And man does not know how to stop. The wealthy are especially unable to stop their irrational and endless accumulation of wealth. Rarely does a rich man reach a point where he says that he has earned enough and can stop now. He is more likely to continue working tirelessly to amass wealth until he dies. After having spent much of his life obsessing over money, his self worth is closely tied to his net worth. He can no longer extricate himself from a lifestyle of obsessive money making. He had always told himself that one day he would have made enough and then he would be all set for a happy life. The truth is, he enjoys earning money even more than spending it. An even bigger truth is, when man is caught in the grip of an obsession, he cannot be truly happy.

Here's where things stand then with regards to money and its impact on man. If he is dirt poor, of course it helps to ease his daily suffering. If he struggles to hold things together from one paycheck to the next, more money may indeed relieve that stress. Past this stage though, increasing wealth may have no effect, especially if everyone else in his social circle also gets wealthier. Perhaps if he is substantially wealthy relative to his peers, he may indeed report deriving slightly more life satisfaction owing to his higher status. Yet, this increase in well-being is in a tiny realm of his life, the financial realm, and may well be outweighed by other factors that also contribute to overall happiness. His obsession with wealth can make him quite miserable. In other words, it's complicated. In the end, to man's continual surprise, more money doesn't do a whole lot to make him happier.

Of course, all this careful reasoning may fall on deaf ears. Man, if somebody gave me a million dollars, I'd quit my job right now, move to an island, and sit at the beach drinking cocktails all day. Heck yeah, I'd be happy. So says practically everyone. As straightforward as this line of thinking sounds, the fact of the matter is, human brains just aren't wired to stay happy from an infusion of wealth. Even presuming one can consume sugary cocktails all day without descending into alcoholism and diabetes, there are other factors that will pull his state of mind back to his baseline. He will adapt to his new wealth, of course. In addition, in the new island setting, he'll be faced with a few sobering realizations. He has to make friends all over again to replace those that he lost, and he doesn't know if he can trust those who befriend him, now that he is a rich target for crooks. The natives may not exactly welcome the new millionaire in their midst with open hands, and maybe they even resent his presence. To make things worse, he's getting fat and lazy from having nothing to do, and he has to push himself even harder to run every morning to lose the calories from his island lifestyle. He is even more purposeless now that he doesn't need to work to pay bills. At times, he finds himself wishing he could go back to those good old times with his old buddies.

What exactly makes money so sacred to modern society? Anthropologists like to talk about the dominant cultural practices of a set of people living at a certain time. These are the rituals, customs, or beliefs that shape society. The Catholic church and its edicts dominated Europe in the middle ages, and influenced everything from the art and science to the literature of that era. For the ancient Egyptians, the concept of afterlife and immortality were major cultural obsessions. Accompanying this were rituals like mummification and the construction of those massive tombs for their dead God-kings, the pyramids. Similarly, seafaring and exploration was the essence of life for the ancient Polynesians, and this led to them build boats capable of traversing the oceans and to develop a deep knowledge of stars and navigation.

Money

The unchecked growth of a dominant culture leads to monoculturalism, which is the suppression of all other cultures in favor of the dominant one. The Nazis tried to create a monocultural society by force. Pre-war Japanese society was a monoculture that grew out of active preservation of traditions coupled with the exclusion of external influences. Today we have reached dietary monoculturalism, with most of the world getting its calories from just a handful of grains such as corn, wheat and rice, where previously there used to be hundreds. A similar dynamic is at play with the smaller languages and dialects of the world dying out and being replaced by English or other major dominant languages that each newer generation preferentially adopts.

Man today lives in a monoculture of money. His life is dominated by its pursuit. Nothing else comes even remotely close to competing with this uber-culture. A sociologist visiting from another planet would call earth a stark world ruled by cold economic considerations. Everything is described in financial terms and monetary values. Man is preoccupied with thoughts about money. How much he has, how to get more, who has it, who doesn't. It wasn't always like this, but it is how it is now, and those winds of change are blowing faster. All decisions are made only after due consideration and respect is paid to the all powerful God of Money. This is who he has become, and he has forgotten how to even think of life in human terms. To escape the evil associated with money, to be human, he must continually resist the God of Money, and the tunes that it has him and everyone else around him dancing to. He has to see through the illusion of happiness it creates. Of course, man is a social creature, and resisting the herd and going against his group will never be easy. He needs his own strong internal culture that is based on what it means to be human and to be alive. How he can develop this strength then, is the million dollar question.

Power

If you want to test a man's character, give him power.

- Abraham Lincoln

Power itself does not corrupt. Fear corrupts. The fear of a loss of power.

- John Steinbeck

Every child takes great pleasure in knocking over a stack of blocks. The thought forms in his head even as the blocks are being put together. Then his hand reaches up and converts that thought into action. He smiles with delight as he watches the tower topple with a crash. The world has been changed according to his wishes. Man has a fundamental desire to modify his surroundings according to his designs. He applies transformational pressure to material objects such as sticks and stones, as well as to creatures that may resist his motives, such as plants, animals and other human beings. Power is a measure of his ability to translate his wishes into reality and influence the world.

Expressing his power, by wishing for something to change and then doing what is needed to effect that change, is the purest source of pleasure for man. He simply loves making things happen. The entire manmade world is a vast testament to man's love of power. Skyscrapers, bridges, dams and highways are monuments erected by the will of powerful men who command other men to move mountains of earth in the name of progress. The massive pyramids, the sprawling temple complexes and the towering cathedrals commissioned by God-kings of the past were similar demonstrations of power. The art, books, music, inventions and discoveries of man all serve to inflate the power of the creator, and drive him to create even more. By the same token, man's power fixation is equally responsible for all the wars, tyrannies, despotism, torture regimes, genocides, terrorism and criminality that this world has seen.

As every child soon learns, there are limits to man's ability to realize his wishes. The constraints of his life, the laws of physics and nature, and especially the will of other men, all oppose his intents. This does not stop him from trying, and he engages in a lifelong struggle to achieve what he wants. When he fails, frustration often results. When he succeeds, at times he takes satisfaction in the results, yet on other occasions he does not even notice that he has gotten what he had sought, since he already took it for granted that he would get what he desired. Such is the nature of man and his relationship to power.

At the lowest levels, power relates to essential human rights. When man is denied the ability to do absolutely anything at all, to do as he pleases from moment to moment, he is rendered helpless and vulnerable. Total helplessness implies zero power, or the inability to control one's basic circumstances. No man enjoys being in this state for long. Consider the situation of a kidnapped hostage in shackles. The only thing he can control is his thoughts. Important as the ability to maintain internal calm is, it does not change the facts of his condition. When such a man regains even a tiny level of control, such as being able to shift his feet every few hours, his sense of wellbeing is lifted immensely.

THE ETERNAL SEARCH

Slaves and prisoners are also denied power. The stated goals of imprisonment are crime deterrence, keeping society safe, allowing the convict time to reflect on his act, or ultimately, rehabilitation. However, the primary effect of prison on the incarcerated man is a drastic reduction of his freedom for the time he is behind bars. Every detail of prison life is highly prescribed. The system and the guards control everything for the imprisoned man, from the time he wakes up to the time he goes to sleep, from what he eats to when he eats, from his choice of clothes to his choice of cellmates. Prison serves to punish man by taking away his right to do as he pleases, thus curtailing his power and his happiness. One can find happiness while in prison, but that is simply a testament to the human ability to adapt, no matter how harsh the conditions. Indeed, the more sadistic amongst the prison guards understand this well. When faced with a difficult prisoner, they will vary the rules and routines arbitrarily and unpredictably, to keep the target of their attention from ever adapting.

When given a choice, any imprisoned man chooses freedom over continued jail time. A free man is only nominally free though, and only relative to being imprisoned. Rules, restrictions and constraints will still apply to his life, arising from his interactions with his family, friends, society, employers, law, government, beliefs, nature, etcetera. Man craves power because of the increased freedom it promises. Power allows people to live lives closer to their ideal, and choose a more authentic self. This is true whether one is a mob boss or a mother of three children or an artist. Man will thus choose his own unique brand of relative power according to his definition of an ideal life. Often, this involves trading one aspect of life with another to get closer to the ideal, and get more power along the preferred dimensions. To a mob boss, power is his ability to command respect and fear, to run an efficient organization, and to ruthlessly eliminate his competition. In pursuing this ideal, he will risk jail time, he will give up his ability to walk the streets unprotected, and he may sacrifice any expectations of living a long life. The artist might crave the ability to devote himself fully to creating art, without restriction, without worrying about jobs, bills, chores and obligations. Towards this end, he may end up without a car, money for nice meals, a clean room, or a steady girlfriend. The mother who seeks to be the perfect parent, always available and attentive to her children, may have to decide that she can't simultaneously be that and a star performer at her demanding job.

Man's pursuit of relative power along his chosen dimensions leads to specialization of work skills and refinement of culture. This is a chief part of the engine that drives civilization. It is this frantic accumulation of a personal brand of power that allows for progress to happen. His need to stand out with his own brand of power is responsible for all the richness and variety of life in modern society. If early man hadn't chosen to trade one sort of power for another, all of his kind would all still be mostly identical apes on the savannah. Each individual ape being very accomplished at feeding himself and generally being a well-rounded ape, but nothing more.

Leaders of men are those who are able to use their power to persuade other men to do as they desire. Naturally, the men may not want to do what a leader wishes them to do. They may have planned to do something else completely, and here is this person telling them what to do. This creates conflict, and to dissipate the tension the leader must convince the men that his goal is their goal too, that they share a common intention. He must thus inspire, guide, motivate, aid, oversee, reward, and punish the men he seeks to control. Often, he may deceive and trick them into believing something that is not true. Irrespective of how he enlists them, a good leader commands the attention of his men, and enjoys the satisfaction of diverting their energies towards achieving common goals. The thrill of having complete trust and genuine respect from even a handful of capable others is without parallel.

To be leading implies to be standing out. A leader cannot blend anonymously into the group. His is a lonely and isolating position to be in. He cannot truly be friends with the men he leads. He cannot choose to be simultaneously well liked and well respected, because he will often find himself in opposition to his men. He must push them where they don't want to go, and sometimes he must set an example. He must stand up to face the elements when the others can duck for cover. He cannot be passive. He must constantly engage with people who are in opposition to him and deal with hard facts that need to change. When the group fails at a task, eyes may well turn to the leader and imply that it was he who failed. To lead means having to deal with this threat on a constant basis. Essentially, this requires a willingness to stick one's head out, withstand failure and embarrassment, and recover from it. Two kinds of men succeed in doing so. The first are those who have the humility to admit their mistakes, the strength to learn from them, and the courage to try again. The second are born psychopaths, who never admit to their mistakes, who feel no remorse for misleading and manipulating others, and who have no scruples to prevent them from trying again.

Leadership is associated with being powerful, but the two are separate things. Power can be inherited, transferred, usurped, bought, or simply lucked upon. An entire nation can be misled to elect a person incapable of leading them as their president, the most powerful man in the country. Money can be thrown around by puppeteers working behind the scenes to help elect such a misfit. The son of this president may then inherit his power. Another fool of a man who happened to go to college with the president's son may end up with a share in this power, and so on. Power spreads without the slightest regard for merit.

Power

In contrast, leadership is a trait that one is partly born with, and partly acquires over a lifetime of learning through mistakes. The ability of a man to lead is irrespective of how much power he possesses. Since power is relative and depends on the context and setting, any man has the potential to lead. When a yacht full of high flying financiers and powerful executives catches fire in rough seas, the lowly deckhand who stays calm as he organizes the frantic suits into orderly groups and instructs them on how to unfold and board the rafts safely, he is their leader. Not any of the formerly powerful men who now scramble for their lives, nor the captain if he happened to jump into the first available raft and paddle off.

Since almost every facet in life involves rubbing against the desires of other men who may have different or competing goals, basic leadership is essential to building power. A man must thus choose continually and carefully if he wishes to lead, who he wants to lead, when he wants to lead, how he wants to lead, and where he wants to lead them to. He cannot possibly be a leader in every dimension and for every occasion. Often times though, he does not choose the optimal arena to play in, or the right dimensions along which to build and exert his power. Maybe he chooses the wrong career, or he succumbs to peer pressure and does things that he normally wouldn't have preferred to do. When this happens, he is deviating from the pursuit of an authentic self that is optimal for life satisfaction. He may however hesitate to correct his course, because he has gone too far down one road, and is too afraid to lose all his power and start from scratch again. For instance, after being promoted at a job that is not a good fit for him, he may be tempted to continue at that same job because he values the extra power for the sake of power alone. Of course the longer he stays, the further away he gets from what could be his true calling.

Decision anxiety is the price man pays for his power to choose between a variety of life options. Every time he gives up something to gain something else, the loss hurts. At times, this sort of situation can lead to a sort of paralysis that spills over into other aspects of his life. He begins to let what he can't do interfere with what he can do. For instance, a man who craves the energy, nightlife and potentiality of living in a big city, while simultaneously yearning for the quiet beauty, clean air, and freedom of space of country living, may indeed make no effort to even pursue either option, and instead get comfortable with a routine that locks him up in the suburbs. Instead of accepting the opportunities to go into the city and meet with friends on occasion, or going on hikes into nature when time permits, he may stay indoors in his house and complain about how he's stuck in the suburbs.

Whenever man decides between two competing options, he resents making those trade-offs. He does not want to have to decide. He wants it all. This is the mobster who wishes to be the king of the underworld and yet above the law, or the politician who flouts every law in the book and yet wants to be known as the most beloved leader of all time. The desires arises for absolute power. Absolute power is the ability to live life as one wishes, and to control one's fate without having to make any of those painful trades. One despises the restraints that still remain. Experiencing much power leads to an urge for even more power, or absolute power, in an attempt to finally achieve actual control. As they say, absolute power corrupts absolutely, because in its pursuit, man is attempting to break free from all obligations, without regard for good or evil.

Power acts as an amplifier for man's inherent nature. If he is flawed, power magnifies the flaws. In this sense, man can do great good or evil proportional to his power, and herein arises the responsibility that comes with power. Of course, he tends to resent being held responsible for his actions. He wants the goods without the guard duty. He wants no strings attached to his power. It is when he forgets or acts indifferent to his responsibility that his power is directed towards creating evil. This is especially true when he is entrusted with safeguarding the wellbeing and the lives of others, whether he is the pilot of a jumbo jet or the president of a nation. These are the men that society expects and relies on to act with utmost responsibility, because when the fail us, the consequences are large.

Even a powerless man can boost his sensation of power, at least for a short while, simply by acting irresponsibly, the consequences be damned. When he is desperate for power, he is tempted to manufacture it for himself out of nowhere. In perverse fashion, he digs a deep hole in the dirt to shield his mind from accepted norms of good and evil, from where he can completely disregard everyone and everything else. The man who plants a pipe bomb in a supermarket now holds in the trigger great power, but only because he has disregarded his basic responsibility towards fellow humans. Yet, it's not just powerless men who resort to acting irresponsibly to feel powerful. The leaders of men have been known to start wars just to renew their claims to power. Their behavior is similar to that of a mentally unstable man with the button to a nuclear weapon, who can simultaneously claim to possess infinite power and zero responsibility for his actions.

Psychopaths are those who act to exert and abuse their power indiscriminately, without regard for harm caused to others. They are able to suppress the empathy that man normally feels when witnessing another suffer. The psychopath's greatest ability is to not feel distressed by situations that he himself would surely suffer from experiencing. In other words, even a psychopath feels another man's pain or distress, but he is able to turn that emotion off, depending on what's at stake for himself in terms of costs or incentives. Not surprisingly, wherever sizeable temptations exist, psychopaths flock like wolves at a kill, abusing their power to manipulate, defraud, neglect, abuse and harm others. Indeed, the majority of crime can be attributed to repeat offenders who measure high on psychopathic tendencies, and for whom the uncertain risk of getting caught and receiving prison time is not a sufficient deterrent if the rewards from crime are more certain and high in value.

Most men are not psychopaths, and only a small portion of criminals are psychopaths. However, all men do have psychopathic tendencies in varying degrees. Like a child, he entertains fantasies of life with no internal controls, where he can act without having to deal with the voice in the head. Suppression of one's own distressing emotions is a useful trait, and can be learned over time, as evidenced by the common avoidance reaction of folks who encounter a homeless person on the street for the thousandth time, as compared to the first time. It is just as simple a matter as turning one's face away, so that one isn't confronted with the distressing emotion, and all is good. The challenge for man is that he himself is the observer of his own actions. Every time he ignores the reality of a situation and suppresses a true emotion, there is a part of him that must make a note of that act of suppression. If power is the ability to live closer to one's authentic self, then a life full of suppressed emotions cannot be true to that ideal.

One's perception of power often differs from reality. Typically, man believes himself to be more capable than he actually is. The average man reports himself as possessing above average skill and competency, which is a statistical impossibility. His perception of his own power is thus frequently subject to correction from external forces. This could be in the form of criticism from other men, such as an insult or an act of disrespect. Or, this could be via the objective results of some endeavor, such as failing at a test or performing poorly at a job. Irrespective, when he receives this negative feedback, it takes a hit on his self esteem. With his power diminished, he feels smaller, as if a part of him has died, and this causes him much discomfort. To make himself feel better again, he seeks someone else to blame. Only rarely does he fault himself, for doing so does not relieve his pain effectively. After all, if he holds himself responsible, he cannot externalize his sadness and anger. More likely, he blames the person or thing that diminished his power, or else, the world at large. The very next step he takes after assigning blame is to seek revenge, by lashing out blindly at those he feels have attacked him. The result is violence.

Threats to man's inflated sense of power are thus one of the chief sources of interpersonal violence, and more generally, of the evil that one associates with power. A high or low self esteem by itself does not correlate with violent and hostile behavior, but having a fragile self esteem certainly does. This fragility is highest amongst men whose culture strongly values taking pride in oneself at all costs. If one is expected to hold his head high no matter what, of course the circumstances will on occasion win out and beat the man down. He may already be straining to hold things together after the stress of a long day filled with rejections, insults, and reminders of his low status. The slightest hint of disrespect or a harmless question or comment may push him over the edge. The fall from his perceived power level to his reality is pretty steep, and he snaps. Those who are closest to him then bear the brunt of it, because they are the only ones he can subject to his violence without fear of retaliation or drastic consequences.

An added dimension to power today is fame of the digital kind. This is essentially power in the hyperconnected internet world. Such fame translates to direct influence over the thoughts and behaviors of virtual followers, which essentially power. Much power can be leveraged from the ability to lay claim to the tiniest fraction of attention from strangers across the planet, as long as these strangers count in the millions. Compared to famous people in the past, fame today is earned and lost much more rapidly than ever. The fickle nature of fame drives the fame seeking man to obsessively track his own tracks. He is caught in an endless loop of performing a small piece for the crowd, and immediately checking the impact of his performance on the crowd's mood and attention. Once man has defined himself in this way, it is hard for him to escape his own definition without risking a total loss of identity. Furthermore, the mechanisms for achieving digital fame seem on the surface of it to be available to anyone who has the right stuff plus a good amount of luck. This tempts man to try endlessly, playing the fame lottery. Most men will fail to make it at the name game. Yet, millions will spend much time and effort nevertheless in these virtual popularity contests.

Taking advantage of the desire for fame in the masses are other power hungry men, the young doyens of technology. Ambitious, aggressive and arrogant, yet polished in their manners and appearance, these men typically arise from affluent suburbs, pass through the turnstiles at an exclusive university, and join or form software firms, where they lay the framework of the sticky spiral threads of the giant spider webs of social media that entrap the entire planet into their digital creations. In seeking out their human prey, those future internet addicts aptly referred to as users, these self-promoting men and their parent corporations proclaim noble aims of improving the lives of others and making the world a better place. The guiding principle of their work though never varies, which is to maximize the hold of their product on the addict's mind, which is subtly leveraged at a later date to extract cash streams from the addict.

Much of what is true for money in terms of its effects on man applies equally well to power and fame. To a certain extent, these three commodities are interchangeable in society. If a man possesses one of the three, he has a fair likelihood of eventually gaining the other two, or he can exchange one for another. In addition, the adaptation process works just as well for power and fame. Power in a social context represents man's ability to have influence over other people, and to get them to do his bidding. Unlike money, which can sit passively, power is by its nature a dynamic. Adaptation is even more likely to occur every time one exerts power. When they say that power corrupts, it is the adaptation process that is being referred to. Once he gets used to ordering people around, it's hard to deal with not getting his way. He is so attached to this brand of power that he continually fears its loss, and fights viciously to retain it at all costs.

Once upon a time, power was intimately associated with exceptional merit. The primitive was self-sufficient and fiercely egalitarian, with everyone in the tribe essentially possessing the same basic capabilities. If any one man in the tribe was bestowed with extra power, it was because he had demonstrated extraordinary courage, competence, wisdom, or leadership in the past. Perhaps he had saved the tribe on more than one occasion with his hunting prowess, his dedication, his ability to settle quarrels, or his superior decision making. Nevertheless, the primitive tribal leader's cache of power was fragile and fleeting. It required ongoing effort to renew, and the stress of maintaining and defending the top position from other contenders took a toll. He might have tried to cement his power with a network of relationships to other powerful men, but even this required much astuteness to navigate and much continually vigilance against treachery. Since it was not possible for primitive man to accumulate excessive wealth and then use that as a means to concentrate power, there were limits to his influence, and these limits were based precisely on his merit. In contrast, modern society allows for unlimited wealth concentration, and thus allows for power to be bestowed upon unexceptional men.

The question remains, whether it corrupts man or not, does power brings him any lasting happiness. Of course, when starting from a state of complete helplessness and lack of freedom, adding power gives control back to man for his basic rights. Beyond that, man is always trading power along one dimension for another. The dilemma this presents him with causes him to seek out even more power, and aspire for absolute power. He must distribute the power that he has carefully amongst his chosen dimensions. There is always a balancing act to be performed. Certain folks have nearly unlimited access to power, wealth, and sex. Still, they have limited quantities of the invariants of the human condition, which are life span, health, and time for loved ones. Paradoxically, they spend the things they have in limited quantities, like time, chasing after things that they already possess in near unlimited quantities, like power, because their identity is so strongly defined by the things they have a lot of.

Many a billionaire may pledge to give most of his money away, but he does so not all at once, but over the remaining decades of his life. In giving to his preferred charities and foundations, and dictating what they must do with those endowments, he retains power. He is just trading one sort of power for another. No billionaire ever says he will give up his power along with his money too. Until the day he dies, he prioritizes his power over all else. Nevertheless, the ability to live one's life as close as possible to the one's ideals does bring some life satisfaction, provided one can avoid the corrupting influence and entitlement effect of power.

Ultimately, excess power alienates man. If he chooses to climb a pyramid, it will be lonely at the top because by definition a pyramid narrows toward its apex. There is not enough space for everyone, and the higher one goes, the fewer folks one meets. In climbing as high as possible, he will have surely trampled

Power

over the desires and ambitions of a few. Often this involves machinations and scheming, which makes him no friends. Even when it is simply his ability, perseverance or pure luck that propel him to the top, there are others who had to make way for him. These surpassed men then have to lower their estimates of how high they themselves have climbed, because the summit is always assessed relative to what one can see when one looks upwards. This may cause them to resent the powerful man, such that while there is much respect and admiration shown externally, both parties know not to confuse that with true friendship.

Seeking power just for the sake of power invariably makes man unhappy, either in the process or due to the consequences. It is far better that he identify the dimensions of power that he cares about, and work to improve along those. He can then focus on things he can control and get things done, one small step at a time. As he builds a lifetime of work, he must help others around him as well, so that he brings others to the top with him to keep him company. Ultimately, when man has the wisdom to define an ideal, and if carefully cultivated power gives man the freedom to live his life closer to this chosen ideal, then he can be true to himself. That is a recipe for an authentic life filled with satisfaction for the choices he has made.

Sex

Everything in the world is about sex, except sex. Sex is about power.

- Oscar Wilde

Sex is the consolation you have when you can't have love.

- Gabriel García Márquez

There's always a top and a bottom for sex. This is often true for the positions themselves, but it is always true for the participants and how they perceive the sexual act happening between them. Even when it is approached sideways amongst near equals, there are dual roles to be played. Somebody takes, and somebody gives. Somebody is happy, somebody is not so happy or outright unhappy. A distinct power dynamic is involved with every sexual act, as illustrated by Oscar Wilde's quote. What is it about sex between two people that makes it so different from those same two people meeting to get lunch?

Sex is an act of intimacy between two lovers, or sex is a routine act of play between partners in a connected relationship, but just as frequently and simultaneously, sex is a transaction conducted in the currency of power. Somebody is receiving a bit of something for himself, and somebody is letting the other have it in return for something else. There could be any number of reasons why two individuals come to engage in the act, but during the act itself, man is fundamentally asserting his claim to what he believes he is entitled to. The consequences of man's entitlement to sex are vast, and have shaped and influenced nearly everything that seen in society and culture. Love makes the world go round, but sex makes the world spin like a top and go absolutely bonkers.

And man, does man like to fuck. Like a dog, he's at his happiest digging in the dirt and chasing around for a bone. All he really wants to do is fling his whole body about, move all that sweating muscle without going anywhere, back and forth, in and out, on and on. Just like that dog again, you can kick him, you can beat him, but you can't cure him of this obsession any more than you can get that dog to let go of the bone. The house may be burning to the ground, the plane may be going down, his entire world may be crumbling down around him, yet man does not care. Dying salmon on a gravel bed pumping to discharge sperm and spawn eggs in their last gasping moments of life doesn't come close to describing man's obsession. All he wants to do is just fuck fuck fuck.

So do women, but usually they're pretty good at hiding it.

A tangle of traits drive attraction to the opposite gender. This is a thorny and contentious issue for both men and women. Both cynically accuse each other of being shallow and manipulative. The actual picture is complex, and each gender's requirements depend on whether they seek a short or long term engagement. For a short fling, when all a man seeks to do is spread his seed and move on, he is primarily interested in fertility cues in a woman. These are traits such as her body's proportions, especially of her waist, hips and breasts, her facial features, her hair and skin, her youth, her athleticism, etcetera. Things are at their simplest and most predictable in this scenario. All he cares about, as dictated by the genes honed over his evolutionary past, is whether she will bear healthy and attractive children from his seed, and be able to nurse them to adults who can propagate further. He fully knows that he is choosing to mate based on highly superficial, at times blatantly fake visuals, but he cannot help it. His sexual desire for attractive women is not rational. His only choice is to whether to act on his desire or not.

If, on the other hand, man is genuinely interested in her for the longer course, then in addition to the superficial characteristics, he may also care about her intelligence, her humor, her kindness, and other personality traits. In making these judgements, he wants to make sure that in addition to her obvious fertility potential, she is someone he will enjoy spending time with, and that she will be a caring and considerate partner, at least for the duration that they stay coupled and perhaps raise children together. Naturally, a woman who seeks a man primarily for a short term fling will emphasize her superficial characteristics with clothes, jewelry, make-up and bodily enhancements, while one who is in it for a longer relationship will play up her personality and charm, and may even downplay her physical attractiveness on occasion to simply to test the man's commitment to her.

For the woman, short term flings are essentially about how they make her feel, rather than the man in question himself. In order to feel good about herself, she prefers to have sex with a man whose choosing makes a careful statement validating herself. For instance, she may make a short stand with a famous man who may have many females to choose from, and by the act of picking her, he automatically deems her as special. Or, she may sleep with a powerful yet busy man, who once again makes her feel special by giving her attention from his precious time. Or, she may swoon for the hot pretty-boy or the fit, rugged individual, whose excellent genes proclaim themselves loud and clear to her. At times, she may let an inexperienced younger man copulate with her, simply to enjoy the sexual energy and undivided attention that he ravishes upon her while he idolizes her as a Goddess who is the epitome of fertile womanhood. Finally, she may go for brash, abrasive and rough bad-boys, and at the extreme, even criminals and serial killers. Her emotional calculation here is that such men show normally no compassion or care towards most of society, but once again they make an exception for her. Thus, they prove her as extra special and desirable, and worthy of practically anyone's attention. Of course, she is usually quite aware of the irrational and even dangerous nature of her attraction to such men, but she just can't help herself. There were many in her ancestral line born to women who made such choices in the past. To lessen the risk of being left alone with an infant and no support to help raise it, women are likely to pursue these liaisons on the sly, and while they are in a committed relationship with someone else.

For the longer term, the woman has to choose more carefully, since she will need to spend extended amounts of time with the man, which is always a challenge especially given the binds of marriage. She still values good genes in the man, as they express themselves in her mate's athleticism, height, and fitness, which in turn will transfer to her offspring. In addition, she wants to ensure that the man is responsible and will support her and the family. The scenario she tries desperately to avoid is to be abandoned with a helpless infant to care for. At the same time though, she wants someone who will give her the freedom and space to pursue her own interests. She does not want to be dependent or feel controlled. Therefore, she tries to choose emotionally strong and mature men, who are caring, good-humored, generous, and show the commitment to lead them both to a better place in life. Yet, she often finds herself unable to stop there. The gold-digger label exists for a reason. Although a woman can resist making her mate choices purely based on his wealth, she invariably finds it alluring. When what she seeks is to feel absolutely safe, secure, and free, there is a thrill in entering a liaison with someone with money or power to obtain a share in that. It may not matter to her so much if the man himself is not inherently attractive, competent or caring, as long as she can rely on his riches to compensate. She isn't so much into the man himself, but his money or power, and she can't help being attracted to the idea of what that does for her.

It is commonly presumed that sex is pleasurable, and that's why man pursues it. Of course, sex can be a whole lot of fun. Two lovers who are totally engrossed in lovemaking can spend hours in complete sensual bliss, melding minds and bodies with the other person, and enjoying endless cycles of building up sexual tension and then releasing it. Man especially is designed to procreate effortlessly, and evolution has ensured that a burst of pleasure arrives towards the conclusion of sex, so that he finishes the act and spreads his seed. Sure, that joy is intense, but it is fleeting. To say that the drive for sex is explained by that flash of gratification is a very incomplete characterization of things. The reward from a few precious seconds of orgasm hardly explains all the trouble that man undergoes in pursuit of sex, often to the point of ruining everything else in his life that is good. If it was simply about the pleasure, masturbation would suffice, and always win out over the desire for sex with a partner due to the low costs involved in bringing oneself to an orgasm. The how and why of sexual matters has little to do with that short thrill at the end. To fully understand the act of sex, it is far more illustrative to examine man's response to a lack of sex, and his behavior in the vast majority of time spent outside of the act itself.

When man desires sex but is unable to find a willing partner, he alternates between restlessness, resignation, and indifference. At a certain subconscious and biological level, his restlessness arises from his fear that he will die without procreating. If this was the only driver of his desire for sex though, his behavior would be indistinguishable from that of an animal in heat. Man is far more sophisticated than that. A lack of sex affects him psychologically and emotionally, first and foremost. It makes him feel like dirt, to be rejected. His level of self worth is usually tied so intimately to sexual access that going without it for even a short stretch of time nags on him. He begins to behave in strange and outrageous ways, ways that surprise him even. He feels compelled to mitigate his distress. There are three courses of action he can take. One, he must find ways to cope without sex, by distracting, deluding or numbing himself. Two, he must channel his frustration continually into improving his chances of obtaining future sex. Three, he must find a way to de-emphasize the significance of sex, and focus on other things that allow him to get on with life. These three courses are not mutually exclusive, and they sometimes involve contradictory behaviors, but eventually he lands in a state of equilibrium between still wanting, not wanting, and not caring. Restlessness, resignation, indifference.

The first course of action is coping, that is, coping while still wanting. To take his mind off his frustration, man may seek to substitute for the lack of sex by over-indulging in more readily available pleasures, such as food, alcohol, drugs, television, sports, games, or entertainment. He may also distract himself by diving totally into his work, art or other passions. He might regularly drive his body to exercise to the point of total physical exhaustion or muscle pain, such that even the thought of sex becomes less attractive. He wants his body to feel numb, as that is preferred to feeling the pain of longing. Over time, if the lack of sexual fulfillment continues, he may even succeed in layering such thick defensive behaviors and coping mechanisms to protect his mental state that he may not even be aware of the reason for their existence.

An alternative and common coping mechanism involves self delusion. Faced with a lack of mates, man will paradoxically raise his standards even higher, in terms of looks, personality and other traits in an acceptable mate. Arbitrarily raising the bar allows him to dismiss the vast majority of potential mates without attempting pursuit. In this way, he can explain his own lack of success as a problem of supply rather than personal effort or qualifications. This aloof man is still not getting any sex, but at least it's not his fault. He can just shrug and say that the problem isn't with him, for he is golden, but with the world. His carefully curated potential mates stubbornly and inexplicably fail to appreciate him and his brilliant worth. Once blame has been thus assigned, action can be taken to punish the blamed. This is the process that converts his sexual frustration into anger and hostility towards the world at large.

The second option for a sexless man is to accept the issue, and tackle it head on. He can work to directly improve his chances for obtaining sex. This involves making himself prominently available, and attracting attention to himself with traits that the other gender finds appealing, either inherent to him or applied superficially to his exterior. In other words, he can focus on self development or on image management. He can strengthen his physique and fitness with hard labor, or enhance his appearance with store bought fashion. He can become more outgoing and open minded, or he can practice how to appear to be charming and chivalrous as the need arises. He can acquire deep skills and expertise, or he can accumulate and flaunt money and power. Some of these are straightforward enough, but may involve considerable time and money spent. He thus needs to choose wisely where he invests. Expending much effort with the aim of purely attracting mates may leave him feeling empty, one-dimensional, and lacking a depth of confidence. He may instead want to focus on a range of activities that improve him has a man, with a better sex life being a consequence rather than the primary goal.

Sex

A quicker alternative to trying to improve himself, and a path that involves zero effort, is to lower his standards indiscriminately. He starts by degrading his own perception of self worth, such that his lack of sexual partners is easily explained. When man believes he is dirt, he does not deserve anyone at all, and then all is good once more. He can blame fate for dealing him a bad hand, an ugly face, a poor upbringing, a boring personality, etcetera, which serves to remove any blame from his actions. He is garbage, and therefore no self-respecting person would willingly want to mate with him. Then, since he is garbage, he can drop his standards for potential sexual partners to the floor as well. This opens the door for him to indiscriminately pursue all manner of mates without regard to compatibility or attraction. Intoxication with alcohol or drugs typically set the stage for this sort of faux courtship, which is unfortunately exceedingly commonplace and widespread. Being intoxicated makes him lose his inhibitions, but it also makes it easier for him to later on justify his actions as those of a sloppy drunk man who wasn't thinking right. Any clarity that arrives, arrives in the harsh and sobering light of morning, but by dusk he has forgotten and forgiven himself, and is once again on the prowl for sexual gratification.

When this man finally succeeds in finding sexual fulfillment after a barren stretch, the effect this has on him is immediate. Right after the act, he feels uplifted. His mood soars, because there was at least somebody who was willing to grind hips with him. For a short while at least, he is not garbage. Once the post-coital high fades though, he returns to his old ways of thinking. If he thinks he is dirt, in his careful reasoning, anyone who chooses to mingle with dirt must be dirt as well. If he cannot face the reflection he sees in the mirror, he cannot truly respect anyone who has sex with him either. He avoids the one person who chose to give him a chance, and instead seeks out a fresh partner, one who isn't tainted by the act of association with himself.

THE ETERNAL SEARCH

A final course of action available to man when bent under unresolved sexual pressure, is to strive to lighten that load. The level of significance attached to sex isn't uniform across men, or across cultures. He is influenced by both his genes and his surroundings. What matters is how he responds to these driving forces. By lessening the importance of sex in his life, he frees himself up to focus on other gainful pursuits, such as his creative endeavors, his education, or his passions. These may in turn result in future sexual opportunities, although this is by no means guaranteed, nor the point of his efforts. Indeed, some men may decide that chasing after sex is simply not their thing, especially given the highly competitive nature of mate finding that often forces them into shallow and self-promoting behaviors that attract attention to themselves. They may choose to forego the pursuit of sex altogether as not worth the trouble, and instead dedicate their lives to a variety of creative passions. With the benefit of time and with advancing age, he may indeed completely lose interest in sex. A significant fraction of men can and do live quite satisfactorily in this manner.

A young man typically grows up today steeped in an extremely hypersexual culture. As he matures into manhood, his pride gets tightly bound to his subjective perception of how he is doing relative to others in the narrow domain of his personal sexual life. He has to rely on an arbitrary notion dictated by his culture of how sexualized he should be in his private life. Everywhere he turns, he encounters subtle and not so subtle messages that being a man requires being ubersexual. Success in this realm boils down one thing and one thing alone, which is the number of high quality mates he can attain, without regard to anything else. His peers all seem to be chasing this ideal. As a social creature, he may get swept along by the masses and just do as they do, unless he consciously chooses to swim against the prevailing current or be asocial. No matter how he copes with it, when sex is felt lacking in his life, he may attach an outsize importance to it. He must still act normally, since that is what society expects, and he dare not drive others away with his desperation. His condition is like that of a latent volcano, ready to erupt when the conditions are right. He is primed to act irrationally and impulsively when confronted with sexual symbols.

Commerce and industry tap into this energy, and get him to spend money in exchange for vague, nonsensical promises of sexual fulfilment. A recorded video of an attractive woman that he has never met or will meet, playing out on a screen, can influence him to buy everything from clothing to cars. These visuals are cheap to produce, free to disseminate, and surround him in an endless parade of sexual promise. Typically, they portray highly distorted images of women with exaggerated fertility cues, such as large hips and haunches combined with thin waists, smooth breasts, a youthful face, and unblemished skin. Men are correspondingly exaggerated into freakish caricatures with huge, steroid-enhanced muscles, in a fabricated ideal of masculinity.

Pornography itself is the largest and most obvious source of such visuals. Porn features an endless stream of mostly perfect individuals engaged in various sexual acts. A primitive man who encountered a fertile, attractive and willing woman would have had two choices, yes or no. His decision would have been weighted by concerns such as whether there were hungry lions or an alpha male to watch out for, and whether he was more starving or hurt than in the mood for sex. Viewed from the safety of one's home, porn involves no such yes or no decision. It short-circuits the brain's audio-visual processes to go straight to arousal, but aside from masturbation, porn offers no outlets to release the tension. The arousal is simply too strong to ignore though, and traps man in a limbo state that he is unable to break free from. He is fully aware of the futility of watching porn, but is left helpless by his own sexual instincts. It is only when the fantasy fades, when man emerges from the throes of porn addiction into the harsh light of reality, that his rational side condemns him for his actions. The result on his psyche, predictably, is more gloom and frustration.

Even leaving porn aside, there is no escaping the fact that commercialized sexuality has a tight grip on man, wherever he turns. In most societies, very blatant and straightforward displays of sexuality in public are generally prohibited. To get around this restriction, acceptable cultural symbols of sexuality form and spread rapidly through social media to become universal. These symbols may be completely arbitrary objects that gain sexuality simply by association or implication. For instance, a sports car is considered sexy. Initially, this might have been due to such cars frequently being positioned alongside existing sexual cues, such as a sexy supermodel. Over time though, the symbol is ingrained in culture, and one no longer needs a supermodel standing alongside the sports car to see it as sexy. Other symbols derive from existing sexual cues and build upon them. For instance, tight yoga pants became preferred everyday wear in women because aside from enhancing their rears, the association with yoga symbolizes that the woman adheres to a health and fitness lifestyle, which itself is considered sexy. Irrespective of how the symbols develop, once established they allow man to use their implied sexuality to peddle concepts and goods. The rich man buys the sports car because of its association with sexual fulfilment, and the aspiring model posts pictures of herself in yoga pants because she wants to be noticed. Both media and real life are cluttered with sexual symbols that act as triggers to fuel man's desire.

Sex is the powerhouse of the world economy. Man can readily make food of all sorts available to himself to ease his hunger, he can entertain himself no end such that boredom is not an issue, but since sex with a desirable partner requires willingness on the part of the other, he is driven to prove his worth to his potential mates indirectly with displays of wealth, power, fame, artistry or looks. Like a performing bird of paradise, he must first show off some bright feathers or accumulated jewels or dance moves in order to win a mate. In return, he desires the company of a suitably attractive and personable woman, but some men will accept cheap and transactional encounters with a prostitute as a substitute for true companionship. From the viewpoint of sex as an economic driver, being able to buy sexual release represents a leak in the bucket of productivity. Not surprisingly, every working-class society somehow restrains, discourages or disparages unrestricted access to sex, such as by imposing prohibitions on prostitution or by looking down upon prostitutes and their seekers alike, with the benefit that this sexual energy is instead channeled into productive economic activity. On the other hand, mere enticements to sex, such as sexual imagery, are not restricted at all, since they only add fuel to the fire of sexual desire that then craves release.

They say that prostitution is history's oldest profession, but certainly it rose to greater prominence with the origin of marriage and its concept of forced monogamy. Opinion is divided on whether primitive man lived in polygamous fashion or as monogamous pair bonds. In theory, in the absence of marriage rituals, early man could copulate with any woman he could charm, coax or coerce into sex. This is indeed how things go in certain species of primates such as bonobos. Similarly, a primeval woman could as well have as many partners as she wished, although she might have been slightly more discerning given the burden of nursing and rearing children, and the toll that childbirth takes. Such wild and free promiscuity however is never found to exist sustainably in human societies. Generally speaking, the biology of man primarily prefers to form pair-bonds with a single mate in monogamous fashion, in order to resolve the dilemma posed by the human child's exceptionally lengthy and burdensome development period. During a time period that spans nearly a decade, the human child cannot feed itself, or fend for itself in the wild. The female does not desire to be left without support for the expensive child-rearing period, and therefore carefully tries to choose responsible males who will show commitment towards the family unit. Over time, evolution resolved the tension by predisposing them to mostly prefer serial monogamy.

Whenever men and women formed pairs, it served as a helpful means of escaping the stifling closeness of the others in the tribe. A majority of tribal societies, such as the Yanomami of Amazon, indeed adhere to patterns of monogamy with some occasional extramarital sex. However, when given the chance, both genders will opportunistically follow a secondary strategy of polygamy. Polygyny, or when a man takes several women as mates, is especially favored if the conditions allow for it. Mainly, this happens via the accumulation of wealth or power by a few powerful men. A few tribes, such as the Mosua of China, lend credence to the prevalence of some polgyny here and there, yet there was little room for extreme polygyny in primitive society. Those men who stood to lose out on mates would not tolerate it, because there was no reason to. Primitive man did not accumulate great wealth, and the egalitarian life in the hunter-gatherer tribe meant that no one person would be too incapable or excessively capable of providing for a family with young offspring. Even if marriage, pair bonds and monogamy was the norm, such a life came with relative sexual freedom. It was always an option for any pair of lovers to sneak off into the bushes and do as they pleased.

Then came farming. The earliest of farming settlements imposed a particular burden on a childbearing couple. Farming is hard work. A hunter-gatherer typically finishes his survival-oriented tasks in three to four hours, leaving him free to spend the rest of the day in camp leisure. In contrast, a farmer typically labors from dusk till dawn, at least during the growing seasons. One must forego hunting and gathering for long periods in order to plough the land, plant seeds, harvest the crop, and defend it from pests. Then, after all the hard work, one must safeguard the yield from thieves, robbers, and from those who did not contribute to the labor. The manual plough was an especially heavy and laborsome tool, typically depending on the bigger male to operate effectively. This led to a division of labor, with the man handling the ploughing and heavy lifting while the woman handled the time consuming chores of weeding, processing, and cooking, in addition to taking care of the children and the household.

Consequently, where previously each hunter-gatherer could have survived as a unit of one within the group, it now took two people working together full time to operate a farming household and simultaneously raise the newborn. Monogamy was strongly favored, because it was the only practice that allowed and demonstrated complete commitment to the family unit. If there were two hypothetical farming settlements alongside each other, the one that practised monogamy would quickly outperform the one that did not. Of course, this is not to say that everyone was happy with the arrangement, but what is good for the happiness of the individual is not the same as what prevails in an economic race. Monogamous farming societies overwhelmed all other settlements.

It was only when farming settlements grew larger into villages, towns and cities that polygyny returned. Once technical progress and mastery of agriculture was sufficient to allow for mass accumulation of livestock and property, a few powerful men could rise up at the extent of others and claim more wives for themselves. Women will accept polygyny and share a single powerful man, as long as it provides significantly greater safety, security and wellbeing than the other pair-bond options. The height of polygyny and harem building coincided with the largest kingdoms in the pre-modern world. Extreme resource concentration and imbalances, such as a king and a few powerful men having nearly endless wealth while the peasants struggle to feed a family, inevitably lead to extreme harem building. The Rites of Zhou written for dynasties in imperial China allowed the emperor to have up to 121 women in his harem.

Here now arose the three great religions of the world, Judaism, Islam, and Christianity, each with their increasing elevation of chastity, by equating it with purity and divinity. In the span of a few centuries, the nature of sexual dynamics changed. Celibacy was the highest virtue, marriage became sacred, sex was for procreation only, and adultery was the great sin. Abstinence was in, promiscuity was out. Polygyny and polygamy was outlawed, but of course adultery never disappeared. It simply became something that a few men could continue to conduct with impunity behind closed doors. Typically, nine of every ten men would acquire a wife, and the remaining one might well die alone and childless. Meanwhile, one of those nine might go on to commit adultery at a grand scale, taking advantage of his position of power or wealth. The great incentive for empire building remained unchanged, even if all the extramarital sex went clandestine behind the doors of the mansions and the palaces. On the outside, everything was still chaste and orderly, and married men had sex soley with their equally virtuous wives, and if they didn't they confessed to their sins and all was good. The more suppressed sexuality was at a societal level though, the more it fueled desire in private. The industrial revolution and its technological innovations unleashed these ambitions and its accompanying brand of sexual puritanism upon the entire world, which continues till today in modern society. Sexual desire is strong as ever, repressed libidos cause much damage and dysfunction, and adultery is commonplace, yet promiscuity and liberated attitudes are shamed, marriage is cherished as sacred, and all is good on the surface.

Sex

Within the bounds of a tight and exclusive relationship such as marriage, man potentially enjoys a higher frequency of sex than in an uncoupled state. Where the single man has to find, attract, charm and persuade a new individual each time he desires sex, the coupled man simply has to wait for or set the right conditions of mutual willingness with his existing partner. In this regard, he has the potential to enjoy greater satisfaction from the relationship, yet there are limits to this satisfaction. Sex is like money in terms of the effect its scarcity has on happiness. Not having any at all makes him more unhappy than having some makes him happy. And once he has some, it doesn't make him ever more happier to get more and more. There is a limit to the happiness he can derive from more frequent sex. Furthermore, libidos can be mismatched in timing or frequency, which complicates the sexual dance between the partners. Naturally, there are negative consequences to the relationship if one party desires the frequency to be higher than what the other wants.

What man must be careful to avoid here is a cycle of appeasement. He craves sex, therefore he panders to his woman. Happy wife, happy life, such a man will nod wisely, when what he means is that as long as he doesn't get in her way, she continues to provide him with the occasional sexual release. Their relationship hinges on him keeping her from getting upset. Well aware of the firm hold that sex has on him, she uses that knowledge to her advantage, to control him. Everytime she wants something or wants to get her way with something, she either withholds sex to punish him, or lets him have it as a reward for continued compliance. This reinforces a power dynamic which is detrimental to the health of their relationship, and ultimately, to his self esteem. Of course, women enjoy being cherished and treated like they are special, and there is nothing wrong with a man showering his woman with love unconditionally. However, when sex becomes the transactional currency of these exchanges, they both lose respect for each other. He resents her for making him jump through hoops, but he resents himself even more for acting like the performing circus dog.

The satisfaction that man derives from sex with his partner then heavily depends on having a mutually strong relationship to his partner. If he truly cares about his partner and vice versa, then regular sex validates their relationship. In this situation, sex feels fun, safe and guilt-free, and serves to further strengthen their bond. If, one the other hand, one or both of the partners are in a sexual relationship without any real emotional connection accompanying the sex, then each act of intimacy reminds them of this, whether they like to remember this or not. Thus, in an otherwise healthy young couple in a committed relationship, over the long term, love without sex is as unnatural as sex without love. Both situations are generally undesirable, and point to the presence of other problems in the relationship.

Sexless relationships are relatively common among couples of all ages, despite the importance of sex to an intimate bond. Almost every dating or married pair will suffer from sexless stretches. Sexlessness is true both as a temporary state due to periods of stress, ill-health or discord, as well as a permanent state for all of those same reasons, plus the additional reason that over the years, the couple may have simply fallen out of that kind of passionate love. Once they have gone too long without it, they may get used to their sexless co-existence as normal. A sudden onset of sexlessness often signals other problems in the relationship, because sex is the indicator that blinks out most tellingly. Sexless marriages are more likely to end in divorce, and sexless couples are more likely to split up. However, couples can and do decide to stay together despite a lack of sex or infrequent sex, due to shared responsibilities for children, jointly owned homes, parental pressures, or, simply because they value each other as trusted, loving, and familiar companions.

Indeed, man can and does enter into relationships for a variety of reasons, including practical concerns such as it making financial sense or offering access to a desired lifestyle. Some men hate being alone, and will thus couple up just to have someone to share the rent, to help with chores, and to avoid feeling lonely. Women of impoverished means may seek the protection and comfort offered by wealthier males, and thus entertain relationships where sex is the main glue. Women from conservative backgrounds may form sexual liaisons with wild, exciting and unconventional men in order to break free from their cloistered lives. Such women will tolerate a relationship with a man who has no emotional connection, or is faking it. In turn, the woman will fake an interest in sex until a better option presents itself, in the form of a man who is emotionally available in addition to being charming or financially secure.

Irrespective of why the connectionless sexual relationship formed, once established, it often lingers longer than it should. Or, maybe the relationship formed on solid grounds, but then all ties broke for some reason except for the sexual one. The experience of sex in such relationships is often tainted by feelings of guilt and resentment. The guilt is felt by the one who is faking a connection just for continued access to sex, and the resentment is felt by the other who is letting him do it just to avoid disrupting the arrangement. Or, as the situation flips during sexless stretches, the resentment is felt by the one who is not getting what he believes he is owed from their arrangement, and the guilt is felt by the other for denying him his pleasure. Problems with sex can quickly break up such weak relationships, just as problems with connection can disrupt the sex in stronger couples.

If man views sex as just a means to release tension, then by definition, who the partner is does not matter. Any set of similar limbs will suffice, and bodies become interchangeable. In this frame of mind, anytime there is a slight challenge to his relationship, via conflict or stress, he is tempted to find a 'less difficult' partner. He is under the illusion that there is such a thing as a perfect mate, one that offers him access to sex and demands nothing. He is thus constantly seeking more variety, since the only way to find this elusive perfect sexual partner is to keep searching. Each time he enters a new relationship, his hopes rise. The new partners bring freshness and enthusiasm as they try to impress each other. Eventually though, their energy fades, the pretence ends, and the true selves come out. To his continual surprise and disappointment, each new sexual partner turns out to be merely human, with human needs, and far from perfect. He is back to square one, and the cycle begins anew.

Exploiting these cyclical behaviors in man is the primary way by which digital means of hooking up, known as dating apps, trap him. Once a sufficient number of potential mates exist in a few popular apps, man has no choice but to participate and perform in these platforms as dictated by the algorithms. After all, if he wishes to find a mate, where better to be than where there are millions of potential mates. Then, if the algorithms require him to portray himself in a certain way, he must do so or risk being sidelined by more eager and desperate competitors. He must build himself up and brandish this enhanced image about in order to stand out in the crowd. Men tend to do this with inflated and unrealistic self-portrayals that aggrandize their wealth, stature and character. Women typically may employ deception in how they appear visually, by choosing outdated pictures of their younger selves, or photographs manipulated to make them seem more attractive. Both genders may obfuscate regarding their relationship status or completely misrepresent their true situation.

Everyone is aware of the absurd and fraudulent nature of this world. Yet, all who participate, simply out of fear of missing out, are complicit in perpetuating it. In return for his continued compliance with this arrangement, man enjoys an addictive form of daily entertainment, a cheap means of receiving validation, and the lure of occasional sexual fulfilment. Sex in the soulless context of the virtual dating world is simply a token that can be traded for anything at all in the sphere of human existence, whether it is a quick thrill, relief from boredom, revenge over an estranged lover, or even just a free dinner at a fancy restaurant. It is simply a cold token exchanged in the currency in power. All the glorious drama and dynamism of human sexuality is reduced to a mechanical transaction. One must be prepared to shut off any distressing emotions in order to get through with the act of copulation. Alcohol and other mind-altering substances come to the rescue here, since they simultaneous numb the senses, impair good decision making, and reduce the inhibitions. Not surprisingly, while the superficial physicality of such sex may be fun, it is often unsatisfying at a deep level. There is no joy in waking up next to such a partner, only the sour taste of alcohol and embarrassment, and an urgent wish to disappear and forget that this encounter even happened at all.

Eventually, over time spent roaming the world of dating apps in search of a mate, man conditions himself to be constantly on the lookout for mere signs of sexual promise. He learns to be so attuned to receiving the signals which indicate to him that the other person may be even remotely willing to have sex with him, that this often becomes all he cares about and craves. He is addicted to the mere stimulation rather than the substance. Once he has reached this point, actual sex isn't a necessity at all, since it is often unsatisfying anyways. He may not even carry through with a real life interaction, given its costs. Man's sex life is now confined to his virtual self interacting with other virtual beings in a sham world.

Primitive man likely had a very different relationship to sex. He was not surrounded by virtual enticements on a screen that never led to fulfilment. If he saw an attractive woman, she was there in flesh and blood as a potential mate, unless she was unwilling or unavailable. He then charmed and wooed her, he won her favors with rewards of meat or fruits, or he coerced sex by using the threat or application of violence. Rape has always had a long and sordid history of existence alongside consensual sex. The act violates the fundamental right of control over one's own body, and represents a grossly distorted power imbalance where the rapist has all the power and the victim has none. Power dynamics of a milder sort though applied in varying degrees to influence tribal sexual politics. Some men of high stature in the tribe's hierarchy undoubtedly had greater access to mates, and others had less or none. Irrespective, sex and sexuality wasn't first advertised and hyped up, yet then shamed and restricted, as it is today. Perhaps sex was conducted in private, out of sight in the bushes, like defecation, but certainly it was not inflated out of proportion to its significance. Sex was simply a part of daily tribal life, along with hunting, feasting, dancing, ageing and dying.

Sex led to pregnancy and offspring with a much greater regularity than in the modern world of contraception. A strict understanding of the cause and effect of sex and pregnancy was extremely weak. In a tribe of tightly homogenous people, it would have been nearly impossible to tell with certainty who fathered whom, and neither did it really matter much since everybody in the tribe participated in taking care of all the kids. Sex with multiple partners wouldn't have been uncommon, further muddling paternity. The traditional marriage bind came about only after man began to farm, acquire property, and cared about such things as clear lines of paternity for his inheritance. Men and women walked mostly naked anyways. Two mutually desiring adults simply had to slip away to copulate without worrying about divorce proceedings, or even more so, about positive pregnancy tests, child support payments, and finding daycare.

For the primeval woman too, mating decisions were relatively uncomplicated. She didn't need to agonize to the same degree as modern women do about whether to give in to desire and pursue short term flings, or think carefully about long term outcomes. A separation had no consequence on non-existent things such as shared property, a tangled web of financial obligations, and childcare lasting nearly two decades. In her two majority states of either being pregnant or lactating, since she couldn't get pregnant again, she could choose to consort with practically anyone she fancied, and might have taken on a new lover every few weeks. If the father of her children didn't share meat from a hunt with her, she could get some from one or another lover, and if all else failed she was quite capable of gathering by herself. Then, for the briefest of few months that she exited those two states, say after weaning the youngest of her most recent brood, she would instinctively gravitate towards a suitable mate, preferably a strong, healthy, capable, caring, and responsible man, to form a pair bond with. She and her mate would try to be as exclusive as possible until she became pregnant, to ensure a good genetic outcome, and to secure paternity to encourage the male's help in caring for healthy offspring that would survive to make it past the harsh initial year. Her cycle would then repeat.

In modernity, an extreme concentration of wealth and influence can secure a glut of pleasures of every sort, including sex. Is there such a thing then as too much sex? Famous celebrities may attract spellbound fans who are hungry for their attention, and willingly offer up sex in exchange. Dictators may abuse state powers to coerce or terrorize hundreds of unwilling mates into having sex. Some wealthy may splurge money to buy sex. Irrespective of how they obtain it, when a thing is available in unlimited quantities, its pleasure fades. Enjoyment of sex, like food or wine, can and often is driven to excess. When access to sex far exceeds the body's natural ability to enjoy it, it goes from being a joy to a heroic yet tedious chore. Frustration may not be the issue, but easy sexual access kills the thrill for man. There is no pursuit involved in getting to the prize. He increasingly misses the even bigger prize of genuine emotional connections that make him feel good about himself. It feels empty. The more trivial it is to obtain sex, the more insecure he feels from a realization that his countless mates don't love him or value him as a person. He suspects that it is his money or influence that attracts them, not he himself. He may even say that he doesn't care why they sleep with him, but he does. Man never stops craving validation. When sex is cheap, he feels cheap too.

If sex in the bounds of a connected relationship is already satisfying, can man add some variety on top? What if he tries to hold a strong base with one or more stable partners, and simultaneously pursue sex with others outside of his relationship? Perhaps the connected relationships give him safe and guilt-free pleasure, while the emotionless flings give him a variety of unlimited thrills? In other words, can he have it both ways, and if he succeeds, will he be happy? Not surprisingly, many men have tried to answer this question with choices made in their personal lives. The results are as varied as always. If he tries this without the consent or knowledge of the main partner, he constantly fears destruction of the stable relationship if his cheating is found out. Even without the fear, if he values his partner, then he must feel the burden of guilt for misleading her. If, on the other hand, he has her consent before he seeks sex outside the relationship, he must still constantly make difficult decisions and face the occasional resentment and guilt. He is chasing a series of short-lived bursts of validation, and the thrill always fades quickly. In the meantime, his main partner is left facing the question of whether to wait for him to return, or just leave him for a more faithful companion. There is no free lunch to be had.

Sex

Sex is that most primal of instincts that man just cannot deny. It makes him happy to strip naked and be vulnerable, and then to be appreciated as a handsome and adequate ape, while in the company of an equally good looking and talented female ape. Yes, sex is frequently a power game that man plays, but that kind of sex feels very different from the kind of sex that complements and strengthens love. Sex cannot ever substitute for love, even in unlimited quantities. No man has limitless time in his lifespan on earth, and if he chooses to spend it in a series of purely sexual pursuits and conquests, along with the associated mindless and ludicrous antics needed to constantly attract and then abandon his mates, then that is time from his own life that he has lost for spending in love.

Love

The immature man says I love you because I need you.

- Erich Fromm

No one loves anyone the way everyone wants to be loved.

- Mignon McLaughlin

I don't have to sell my soul
He's already in me
I don't need to sell my soul
He's already in me
I wanna be adored
I wanna be adored

- Adored, by The Stone Roses

Few things in life can inspire man to the extent that love can. He will move mountains, as they say, in the name of love. At the same time, finding true love is the most frustrating endeavor that he will undertake in his life. A lack of love is felt squarely in the depths of his soul as an unbearable void. It is a huge emptiness inside him that cannot be filled no matter what else he pours into it. Whether it is the mother who never loved him, or the fair maidens who spurned him in his youth, or the lover who so cruelly abandons him when he least expects it, or the world at large that is deaf to his wailing for love, man feels the stab deep in his heart. He wants to be adored, and instead he is ignored. He hungers for love, he wanders the desolate woods and the crowded streets alone, he smashes his fists into unyielding walls in frustration, he lies awake in bed sobbing into the black night, he howls at the moon and come dawn at the sun too, all to no avail. He has so many unique talents to offer and so much love to give, but it all does not matter one bit. His loveless existence isn't anybody else's problem but his and his alone. The universe does not care.

As a child matures, a total lack of love hardens him like no other circumstance can. This was of course the situation of the unfortunate children raised in the post-war mass orphanages of the Eastern bloc, places that have been called slaughterhouses for souls. An effectively similar situation can also exist in certain seemingly functional households, where the family appears normal, but for some reason the parents are unable or unwilling to let the slightest expression of love fall upon the child. He is well taken care of in a material sense, but for his emotional needs, he must care for himself and depend on no other, for no other has ever cared for him. Growing up without any real loving figure in his life, he adjusts to that harsh truth, but it comes at a heavy price. To deal with the pain, he must deny it out of existence. This is true not just for himself but also for those suffering around him.

Love is by no means a guarantee in life. Society and culture make a great big deal about the centrality of finding love to enjoy a satisfactory human existence. Despite this, there are no assured avenues for man to find this love, or a stipulation that his love be reciprocated. Being left unloved therefore leaves him to reason that either something is wrong with him, or there is something wrong with the world, or that nothing is wrong with him or the world but it is the concept of love itself that is wrong.

Accordingly, he is left either depressed, angry, or emotionless. No matter his belief and his response, he finds himself at odds with what he hears continually about that simple recipe for a happy life.

Despite the outward pretenses in common culture about the ideal of selfless love, especially the romanticized ideal often seen in fictional depictions, the reality is somewhat plain and sobering. Man loves, primarily because he needs love. His love is rarely a one-sided outpouring of emotion that continues irrespective of whether it is reciprocated or not. Love is primarily the expression of a selfish need for man, disguised as a gift towards others that begs for reciprocation. As illustrated by Erich Fromm's quote, if man gives any love at all to anyone, it is because of what he needs in return. He wants to be universally adored, which brings out the devil in him.

The closest that man will ever approach the ideal of unconditional love is in his dealings with his young. A mother or a father may deeply love and care for the infant, despite the challenge that child-rearing presents. Every infant is born with a clean slate in terms of its history. It does not deserve to be denied love. By the same token though, it has made no claim to receive love either, aside from the mere act of coming into existence into the world. Every man is caught unawares by childbirth, this abrupt appearance of another human form in his arms, and must all of a sudden decide how to relate to it. The infant cannot reciprocate love, yet it receives much unconditional adoration nevertheless. The cooing of an infant may be adorable, but so are its farts and burps and practically everything else it does. It is the parent that confers love unconditionally to the newborn, aided of course by the biological hormones of love that flow in association with childbirth.

Love

Young children are generally jolly creatures who bring irrepressible life and laughter into any situation with their silly and unpretentious presence. In the eyes of the parent, they are objects of pure love. As the child gets older and demonstrates greater maturity and independence, the dynamic shifts accordingly from a one-way adoration towards an expectation of two-sidedness. By the time the toddler can speak full sentences, he is expected to be able to say thank you on occasion, to be polite but also to demonstrate gratitude. Yes, the parent still cleans up after the toddler takes a shit, but it somehow stinks more now, both literally and figuratively. If the child shows proportionate love in return, the parent feels rewarded for his prior efforts. On the other hand, the parent may develop resentment and anger when his love goes unreciprocated or is met with indifference or misbehavior.

Teenagers have a very clear idea of what they want and don't want, but the wisdom and maturity of their decision-making is still developing. This creates a frequent disparity between what they want and what they should want for themselves. Loving a child thus does not always come easy, as it may require the parent to enforce rules and limits that the teen protests. Sometimes, these rules are strictly for the teen's benefit and safeguarding. At other times, these rules are primarily to improve the child towards an unrealistic ideal as visualized by the parent. The child recognizes these attempts at control and rebels forcefully, since growing up is the act of developing independence and then asserting it. Irrespective, when the child withholds any reciprocal love, the parent tends to feel like he has been let down. The betrayal of love from one's own child can last a lifetime, as can the resulting discord. This is the true test of parenting for man, to continue to show unconditional love to the child long past when the child grows old enough to be able to either rebel or reciprocate the love.

THE ETERNAL SEARCH

Early in his youth, he may experience his first of a series of infatuations, what they call love at first sight. He rides that famous rollercoaster of emotions that accompany his falling for some breathtaking creature, who is so perfect that he might not dare to even approach her, for fear of spoiling his pristine fantasy. No matter whether he expresses his feelings openly to his crush or not, he is completely swept up by the emotion. His life is turned upside down. He can't eat, he can't sleep, he forgets things, he abandons his sports and friends, he does silly things, he laughs and cries at the slightest provocation, and most importantly, he interprets every tiniest thing that she does or doesn't do as a sign of her reciprocal love. If he thinks she thinks similarly of him, his spirit soars, and he is on top of the world. If he feels snubbed or ignored, he wants to sink to the bottom of the deepest ocean and be dead to the entire world.

The most commonly heard expression of love in society is a grown up version of this juvenile crush, which is the ideal of romantic love. In its rosiest rendering, two soulmates exist somewhere on the planet, perfectly compatible and furthermore uniquely matched. These two complementary halves merely need to find each other to be happy. This is the genesis of searching for 'The One'. Once they do come together, the two halves are made whole, coalesced together as one in perfect union. The two lovers lose themselves in each other, and they are made complete. No force on the planet can stop this inevitability of fate from happening. In fact, some uncertainty and tension is necessary even, as any barriers that must be crossed before the two lovers can unite only serve make each other seem more attractive yet. The drama before these magnetic soulmates finally pull together is the stuff of a million romantic tales.

It is also a complete fantasy. No individual and no two people can live up to this ideal. In pursuit of this fantasy, however, man creates much of the interpersonal distress, grief and anguish that accompanies failed relationships. The fantasy drives man to seek a half that will take him to glory. He seeks a God or a Goddess mate who shines so brightly that by mere association with the aura of this perfect individual, man can hide his own imperfections and flaws. Since neither man nor his mate is capable of perfection, such an enterprise is doomed from the start. Once the initial obsession fades, man sees that his mate is merely mortal. Every time he sees imperfections in his mate, he sees that as reflecting upon his own image. He resents his formerly perfect mate for letting him down.

Opposites attract, they say. This is however a very narrow truth, especially for anything more than short flings. Opposite personalities tend to be intrigued by some novel traits in each other, but a connection has to exist based on similarities established in the basic attitudes and opinions about life. Furthermore, there may need to be a good match as well for qualities lying along a scale that one looks for in a mate, such as appearance, intelligence, and affluence. A sustaining relationship needs a lot of common ground upon which the enterprise is based. It is these commonalities that allow two individuals to share a life together. Of course, personalities and opinions can vary, which initially make courtship and being a couple fun. In times of conflict, however, it is these same differences that rise up as a source of contention and cause strife in the relationship. Man values all that he has in common with the other person, but he hates having to compromise on his own opinions.

Once or twice in a lifetime, man will find someone who truly changes his world, and brings him immense joy. He may have found his true love, but if he wants to keep the magic going, he must work hard. As opposed to the fantasy of the true love, real love requires man to admit that he himself is not perfect, and neither is his partner. No one person can rescue man from himself, and such a burden is too heavy for anyone to even try to carry. Furthermore, real love is the recognition that one is always a unique individual and always will be, and the same is true for the other in a relationship. One is different from the other, and these differences cannot be suppressed for the cause of the relationship, but rather must be acknowledged and addressed via a mutual compromise. The act of coming together with another person, to share a life lived together, will therefore always involve certain compromises, no matter how seemingly well suited that person may be. It requires continual effort, from both parties, to express their unique selves strongly while working out their differences where it matters for a shared existence. As a reward for this effort, man gains from the personal development that occurs as a result of learning to work with the other's differences. He is a better person because of the other.

The futility of the fantasy of finding true love with a perfect partner, and the difficulty of the work involved in sustaining real love with an imperfect partner, both cause man to dismiss loving relationships altogether. He may instead settle for a series of short-lived, casual-sexual relationships, often with multiple people at the same time. He gets frustrated or bitter, and condemns all members of the opposite gender as flawed and unworthy of his time for anything beyond transactional interactions for his own pleasure. In this state, even when he encounters a well suited mate, he is unable or unwilling to recognize this. He is constantly distracted and closed off to any potential fulfilling relationships. Or, his attention is divided amongst many, and he can always find something or the other that is inferior or lacking in this person compared to the traits of his other options.

Dating in the digital world perpetuates this epidemic of lovelessness, by bewildering man with a seemingly endless choice of potential partners, but providing little incentives for him to actually take the time to connect with any of them. Fundamentally, what man gets by engaging in these virtual interactions is a wholly unreliable signal that a potential mate might be interested in his constructed portrayal of himself, which consists of arbitrarily chosen pictures and words. A tiny fraction of this sort of virtual attention, when received over and over again from tens or hundreds of potential mates, fills up his time and begins to substitute for having the full attention of one individual. He can validate his self worth in a cheap way, without the messiness, expense and hassle of an actual relationship, but also without any true satisfaction. There is always the potential and the promise that it may lead to more fulfilling connection in real life, but the promise is rarely fulfilled because his attention and the attention of all his potential mates is forced to be split across dozens or hundreds. Every time he gets a deeper signal, such as a potential mate taking the time to talk to him beyond a quick flick of the finger, he gets excited that it may lead to an actual flesh and blood interaction.

This happens on a rare occasion, but he and his partner know how and why they met, and that there are millions of potentially even better candidates to explore, so they never form a deeper connection. He is simultaneously like the drunk man who has lowered his standards to dirt, since he hits on practically everyone, and the superficial man who has raised his standards through the roof, since he won't reciprocate with anything genuine to anyone. In this manner, he may bounce from one partner to the next, completely numb and unwilling to acknowledge the human other. Both he and his mate are desperate for love, but they dare not show this desperation openly, because doing so would open them up to rejection and ridicule. The easiest course is to deny the presence and existence of the other's needs, and leave the moment each have gained what they had wanted from the other.

When faced with a lack of love, most often man will attempt to substitute sex itself for love. Or, similar to how he copes with sexual frustration, he may try to distract himself by indulging in substitute pleasures, such as a mindless consumption of food, drugs, entertainment, material goods, etcetera. Alternatively, he may try to numb himself with excessive alcohol, work, or exercise. He may try inflicting physical pain upon himself to give his mind something justifiably real and sharp to feel instead of the dull and shapeless pain of longing. The crucial differences between the pain of sexual longing and the pain of lovelessness are in its intensity and duration. Sexual frustration in man ebbs and flows like the tides. Its intensity depends on such things as his internal hormonal state, the time elapsed since the last time, and external stimuli. Finally, it can be fixed rather easily, at least for the moment. In contrast, the pain of not being loved is constant, pervasive, and can last a lifetime. To his detriment, man is unable to distinguish one kind of pain from another, and often remedies lovelessness with sex.

Marriage, despite the heavy significance afforded to it in the modern world and its frequent association with symbols of love, has little to do with love. Being married is a state largely independent of the state of being in love itself. Love may blossom before or after marriage, with or without marriage. Love may be the cause of or the eventual result of marriage. Marriage may be the cause to blame for love's demise, or marriage may be the result of desperate measures undertaken to prevent love's demise. Marriage may simply be a tax saving measure or a step taken in haste after the woman gets pregnant. Love can exist both inside or outside of marriage, with the married partner or with unrelated partners. The modern obsession with the fantasy of true love culminates with a frenzy in depictions of the perfect wedding ceremony, where as per the fantasy, two soulmates cement and proclaim their love for all the world to see, and all the gathered witnesses cheer and clap, confident in

Love

the soundness and stability of the union. If this were truly the case, a divorce lawyer would not be a thing.

Marriage is simply a highly prescribed relationship structure with a strong tradition and heavy cultural baggage. This arrangement originated early in civilization as a means of securing the pair bond and protecting the resulting offspring. In its modern form, the married couple typically share everything under the roof that constitutes the household, including meals, beds, exclusive sexual access to each other, children, pets, plumbing, electricity, bills, responsibilities, chores, conversations, fights, cars, trips, social engagements, visitors, infectious diseases, etcetera. It is a practical arrangement, first and foremost. Family, society, and government all prefer the predictability that arises from standardization of the marriage norm, such that this norm can be used to take action appropriately. When the marital status that man can exist in are restricted to either Single or Married, with maybe Divorced as an addendum, it simplifies everything from tax filings to dinner conversations with friends and relatives. All one needs to know is which category is publicly true. Checking boxes such as Married But Mostly Friends, Married And Madly In Love With A Colleague, or Married And Chugging Along Just For Kids Sake would only complicate things to no end for both the tax man and the visiting in-laws.

The reality of marriage is more complicated, to say the least. Some would call it a hot mess, but it is simply a reflection of the fact that modern life places too much expectation on marriage to solve all of its problems. Take two well meaning individuals, partner them up, stamp and certify them for togetherness, for life, with nobody to turn to for help but each other, and off they go. They must now set up a whole household by themselves, and live in practical isolation from others in their own home, whether in a tiny apartment or in a large and fenced suburban lot. The more time they devote to the relationship or the family unit, the less time they have for their friends and others, which in turn isolates them further. They must learn to like or at least tolerate each other all the time, instead of just occasionally when they first began dating. They must share money, bills, beds, toilets and chores. On top of this, they must satisfy each other emotionally and sexually, and remain friends too.

A few kids bring more stress with their invariable demands and needs. Human children already have by far the longest developmental periods of any mammal. For a period of several years after birth, they are unable to feed or fend for themselves in isolation, and require dedicated care. Furthermore, the tools needed to navigate society are highly adult-centric, along with rules restricting their access to the young. A child can not or is not allowed to drive, earn money, shop for food, plan its daily schedule, visit doctors alone, stay home alone, sign contracts, and generally make life decisions for itself. The modern child is reared as a heavy dependent, and all systems are geared towards extending a couple's responsibility longer and longer, to the present extreme of twenty years if one includes paying for his college. This has no precedent in prehistoric society, nor in any other animal species.

Couples often stay married even when they derive more unhappiness than happiness from the union. Shared kids and homes, tangled finances, and implicit pressure from family, friends and society may all be the reasons they cannot get themselves to peel apart. Much of this pressure is applied by the couple themselves, who are desperate to avoid seeing all the years they have spent together as a mistake or a waste of their lives. Their culture indoctrinates them into taking a marriage-centric view of relationships, such that being married is the ideal state and being single or separated is lacking something. A divorce is seen as a personal failing, with no regard to whether the decision to stay together for many unhappy years might have alternatively also been a failing. A divorce is referred to as a failed marriage, but being married is never referred to as a failed divorce.

Ultimately though, both parties abandon a high proportion of such arrangements, which should come as no surprise. High divorce rates are simply the visible tip of a problem of monumental proportions that is exceedingly common and widespread, yet kept in private. All too often, they are barely hanging on, biding their time until a better prospect comes along, or the kids are old enough, or simply when sufficient time has passed and friends and family would understand why. In this state, both parties may feel trapped, fully aware of how they would rather go separate ways, but unable to do so. They are like two fully formed individuals conjoined at the hip, wanting to go left and right at the same time and being yanked back. They are like two trees growing beside each other whose roots have gotten entangled far too much for them to separate without killing both trees. The unhappy state may persist for years, until one is released from it by the death of the relationship or of the other, whichever comes first.

Marriage in modernity may evidently then be the biggest joke that man routinely plays on himself. Given this situation, why would anyone choose marriage at all as a course of action? The answer is two-fold. Firstly, hope springs eternal, and ignorance is rife. Every man and woman at the cusp of marriage think that their love is somehow more genuine, since they have thought a great deal before coming to the careful decision to marry. They may therefore believe that they are more capable than all the others that went before them to deal with the challenges ahead. Nobody enters into a marriage thinking that it will end the way it often does. Additionally, the woman typically may desire marriage as a way of securing the man's commitment to the family. Marriage formalizes their bond, which reassures her that he is in it for the long run, instead of wanting to run away. Several states give credence to the greater commitment signified by marriage, for instance in how they divide property and assign alimonies upon its dissolution.

Secondly, man faces pressure from various third parties that encourage him to consummate, clarify and formalize his relationship status with marriage. This wedding pressure is subtle but pervasive, and applies on man from all directions. His parents want him at the altar because they like the certainty of it, and yearn to be able to mark that big milestone off. They may also see marriage as a precursor step to obtaining grandchildren. His single friends may encourage him to get hitched because it gives them clarity as they themselves think about their next life move. His married friends want to validate their own decision as the right one, and will take every opportunity to remind him how their lives are better now. Finally, the taxman will present him with options that show just how much money he could be saving in taxes, if only he would just do the sensible thing and file them as married.

The primitive had no such thing as a highly prescribed tradition of marriage. Life in the nomadic tribe excluded modern phenomena such as an isolated nuclear family residing in a fenced off house, owning huge amounts of immovable property, and sharing a tangled web of obligations. Without external barriers to separation, the primitive's relationships were more fluid and less secure than the modern kind. A couple could break up over something as trivial as a single fight. The tight bond of marriage first originated with the early agrarian settlers, as a joint living arrangement approved and endorsed by others in the tribe. It was a practical setup, designed to allow the newly married couple to work together to meet their basic survival and social needs, and the needs of their newborn. Love, especially passionate love of the sort depicted in fiction, had no place in this arrangement. Companionate love might have developed over the course of the marriage, but it was certainly not a prerequisite for marrying. Indeed, for the most part, the couple had little say in the decision of whom to marry, as this was decided on their behalf by family elders, chiefs, and various interested parties. As is the case now, love and marriage were two totally separate things.

When man is in a committed relationship, even if the relationship is mutually valued and suffused with love, he is not always content. He is afraid of loss, of being deprived of the very thing that brings him joy. He can't bear to be in a relationship without wanting to feel absolutely secure that relationship. This drives him to try to possess his partner, to make her his and only his, and to own her for all eternity. He fears abandonment, of a life spent alone, especially since he depends so heavily on her for his happiness. Abandonment is an ancient fear of man. To be abandoned early in his life by the mother, or to be abandoned early in the course of human existence by the tribe, both resulted in great suffering and death. While he may not suffer physical harm from abandonment by his partner, the mental anguish that he experiences is just as painful and distressing.

Of course, his partner resents any attempt at being confined, just as he himself might resent it. She does not want to be limited in her experience of life. Whenever he seeks to control her and protect her from outside influences, this only makes her want to escape his clutches further, and to do as she pleases. His desire to own her is in direct conflict with her desire to assert her power and live as she wishes, true to herself. In turn, when man looks at something he can't control, it makes him want to control it even more. Whenever she asserts her independence, it rankles him to no end. If she has a busy job and earns a good living by herself, he may fear that she won't need his financial support, and by extension will stop needing him. If she is friendly with her colleagues, he sees competition in the form of more suitable or attractive mates. Sometimes these fears are justified and at other times they are just the constructs of a paranoid mind, but in either case the uncertainty drives him crazy. This is a primary source of friction in the relationship. He loves her but he hates her for what he perceives as toying with his love. Man is tied up in the classic bind, one that compels him to say - I can't live with you, and I can't live without you.

Relationships are not for the faint-hearted. Before man enters into a bond with another human, he had better ask himself if he has the courage to stand alone as a complete person, with adequate strength of personality. If not, he risks becoming dependent on the other for his unmet needs. Perhaps because of how dependency holds couples together even in the face of indiscretions on the part of one partner, it has a well deserved negative connotation. A one sided dependency may be a sign of a power imbalance in the relationship. Going further, mutual co-dependence reveals in both parties an inability to be a well-adjusted individual in their own right. Each relies too much on the other to make themselves happy. For instance, the woman might have an alcohol or drug problem that renders her incapable of functioning in society, but she is supported financially by a man that she cohabitates with. He turns a blind eye to her addiction and even keeps her supplied with alcohol, as long as she in turn tolerates his abuse and philandering. This may of course be an extreme example of dependency, but almost every couple will display some signs of codependency as a result of time spent in a relationship.

A relationship starts with the promise of all the possibilities arising from the mixing of two distinct individuals and their separate personalities. Their early dynamic is like a beautiful young tree with branches blossoming off in crazy directions. Then, in their attempts to unite, to get close and be as one, both parties prune these branches off as wild and unpredictable outgrowths that must be eliminated for the common good. Individuality is curtailed, dependency is built, stability is gained. And then one day, all that remains of the relationship is an ugly stump, and one wonders why it won't bear fruit anymore. If man wants the relationship to continue to blossom, he must let some branches grow. Differences of opinion and conflicts are unavoidable parts of any relationship, and not necessarily unhealthy. They are even to be expected when two strong individuals with different opinions forge a shared existence. The presence of conflict shows that the two still care about something worth fighting for. Difficult conversations can surface hidden issues and result in greater self-awareness. As long as they are willing to engage with each other to address the conflict, they can navigate the rough times and even grow stronger as individuals and as a couple. The tree of their relationship ultimately grows more roots to support the new offshoots.

In the context of an ongoing relationship, the opposite of love is not hate. Hatred reflects the frustration that the other partner isn't living up to their part, perhaps temporarily. Often, a committed couple will vacillate between periods of love, when everything is joyous together, and dark spells of hate, when everything one says or does is wrong and irritates the other. Hatred is emotionally exhausting, and when man can't stand the sight of the other, it drives him away from the object of his hatred. If the hatred were truly pervasive and permanent, then the relationship would have naturally ended, unless there are concerns such as children or finances keeping them together. The opposite of love in an ongoing relationship is therefore indifference to each other. Indifference forms because it allows a couple to persist in the relationship, for practical or expedient reasons, while staying emotionally unattached. An indifferent couple will pretend that everything is normal between them, to avoid having painful conversations. They will also maintain such graces in public, because social interactions are more convenient and smoother when other people don't notice problems and need not be concerned with the chasm between them. An indifferent couple is simply biding their time with each other, waiting around for someone or something to yank them out of the non-relationship.

This someone or something can frequently be a third person. The biology of men never stops being attracted to all potential mates, since he has evolved as the descendant of all those in his lineage who responded to such attractions. However, man has the ability to choose monogamy both with his rational and his emotional brain. Thus, when man is committed to his relationship, he is usually able to ignore the sources of attraction because he logically values the one he is with, and he derives joy from being with his love. If however there is significant external strain on the relationship, or if he feels insecure in his own place and skin, or if the two partners evolve over time to grow and reach in different directions, these alternative options start to appear more and more tempting. This may be especially true for the married couple, since usually there is nobody else they can turn to for the majority of their needs but each other. No one person can satisfy all these dimensions - emotional, physical, psychological, sexual, financial, etcetera - all the time. This is too much of a burden for any one arrangement to carry. The end result may be an affair with somebody outside the relationship.

Roughly three to four years past the birth of their last child, the chances of divorce or breakup in a couple will peak, irrespective of the couple's ages and cultures. While the man always carries within him a slight tendency to stray if the right conditions are present, the woman feels the irresistible pull of adultery the greatest around this time. It is a simple matter of her evolutionary biology asserting itself. Ancestral women stopped nursing their last child around at the age of three or four. After weaning, her hormonal profile changed, she became fertile again, and that is when she sought to seek out fresh mates. Of course, this required pushing out the existing mate, if he was still hanging around. The same periodic effect still exerts its impact on modern couples, much to their bewilderment about why they suddenly find themselves drifting apart. Of course, the more children the couple have together, the greater is the incentive to stay together. Still, the woman may find this period to be most challenging as she is trying to balance being a mother and a wife to her existing family with her deep seated drive to start a new one. Frequently, it is she who is the initiator of divorce or breakups.

Jealousy arises when man fears external threats to his relationship. It is a complex, all-pervading emotion that grips man like a rabid fever and does not let him go. Fundamentally, the jealous man thinks, justly or unjustly, that his loved one will abandon him, despite all the feelings that he has for her and all that he has done for her. He swings between rage, humiliation, and fear, and his behavior correspondingly switches from being angry to becoming depressed to going paranoid. Affairs, the threat of affairs, or even the remotest possibility of affairs all can create immense jealousy. Caught in the throes of jealousy, man is unable to think straight. Night after night, he lies awake sleepless as his mind repetitively runs like a train on the same old beaten track of how could she do this to me. He imagines the fun that they must be having together, and the laughter they must be having at his expense. The same looks, charm, and elegance that he once cherished in her, now form the material for an x-rated movie trailer starring them that loops inside his head. In a sense, he switches from believing that everything was perfect in his relationship, to believing that everything is perfect in their relationship. Not surprisingly, jealousy is the primary cause of violence and homicides amongst two partners a relationship.

Man may grieve the death of a relationship just as much as he might the actual death of the loved one. The loss of love suffuses his day and affects everything he does. He may suffer flashbacks of good times in the past. He is tortured by memories that remind of what he lost and tormented by uncontrollable visions of alternate scenarios where they stayed together, if only they had done this and that. Of course, what he mourns is not the relationship as it was when they broke apart, since it is likely that the cracks already existed for a while. Instead, he regrets the lost potential of their life together, of growing old together. Essentially, the dream for the future is gone, and letting go of that dream pains him deeply.

Affairs have the potential to be ruinous or liberating, depending on the parties and their perspectives. For the cheater, embarking on an affair is a chance to renew life and love, and to break free from the rut of predictability that forms over time in a relationship. The cheater relishes how fresh everything feels in the affair compared to the existing relationship. This is no doubt because both new partners bring energy to the affair. The biology of cheating assists them here, because both the cheating male and the female are both consciously and subconsciously aware that their trysts may not last very long before they get caught. Evolutionary selection history has favored that a cheating couple should succeed in making babies out of just a few intense encounters. Their sexual encounters are thus highly physical, frequent, and intense. Their genitals are supercharged by fear and an opportunistic drive to perform. The male may ejaculate repeatedly in an attempt to secure his paternity within the few chances that he gets with the female. On a mental level, they experience heightened pleasure and bring incredible energy to their secret encounters. They copulate tirelessly and repeatedly. Of course, everything feels surreal and on a different level. If things feel relatively stale at home, it is as much the fault of the cheater as of the cheated upon, or perhaps nobody is at fault. At the same time as the feeling of exhilaration though, the cheater also carries guilt for deceiving, disrespecting and causing grief to the main partner, and fear that everything will be ruined if found out. For the cheated upon, there is immense anguish, rage and distress when the affair is revealed. Their trust has been broken, and it may never fully recover.

Even though man often seeks out affairs to validate his self-worth and to perhaps feel less lonely in his existing relationship, ultimately affairs may have the opposite effect of reducing his self-esteem and further alienating him. He is forever expecting things to end, to be caught and face shame or ridicule, to suffer some consequences for his cheating. There is also the question of the feelings and emotions involved on the part of the person he is having an affair with. Neither party is ever quite sure where all of it is leading to. Whether they talk about it or not, uncertainty is a huge part of any affair. Try as he might to shrug his shoulders and ignore the issue, he knows he can't fool himself forever even if he succeeds in fooling the world. To make things worse, he has to suffer through all his doubts alone. There is typically no one he can talk to about his affairs, at least no one he can talk to while expecting a pat on the back.

In many cases, unless there is some dependency that prevents the aggrieved partner from leaving the relationship, an affair will mark the beginning of the end, but the trouble often starts far ahead of the affair itself. Even if mutual dependency holds the relationship together on the surface, the crack still runs deep in the foundations. The two may never relate to each other the same, even if they stay together and things appear normal from the outside. The pain from the initial discovery of the affair is intense, of course. Yet, it is the ensuing and long-lasting drama of how to move forward from the affair that poisons the ground. It often proves to be simply too challenging for a couple in an already weak relationship to clean up the mess left in the aftermath of an affair in a way that satisfies both parties. For other partners, the discovery of the affair can actually be beneficial. The event sets in motion a re-examination of the relationship and each other's roles in precipitating the affair. If forces them to see each other in a new light, as two well-intentioned mortals doing their best to experience life to the fullest. It may even energize them to devote more time to each other. They may realize that they have been taking each other for granted, and they both share the blame for how things between them lost the shine, became stale, and then finally crumbled.

The reality of the matter is, for any couple, however strong their love might be, the loss of the other is always an imminent possibility. No man can truly control another person. Even if he curtails the other's actions with threats or pleas, he cannot control her thoughts. His partner can always walk away, for any number of reasons, prime amongst them being that as the relationship matures and she seeks more authenticity, she may no longer find value in their relationship. Or, she may simply cease to exist all of a sudden, also for any number of reasons. People die all the time. A realization of this ever-present possibility is deeply unsettling, and threatens the fantasy that he has created in his own mind. He would rather ignore the reality and believe that everything is secure. However, continued consideration of this truth of impermanence eventually brings greater understanding. It makes him value the other. He gains awareness of how his attempts to control his partner, in an attempt to secure his own happiness, backfire by making the other feel trapped. Jealousy and fears of abandonment disappear when one faces the truth that each person is free to walk out at any time, no matter whether there is a third who threatens the relationship or not. He can then acknowledge and assimilate the fact that each moment with his partner is precious, and not to be taken for granted.

Love

A couple who has mastered this truth, about how fragile all human relationships really are, can paradoxically gain strength from the unsettling truth. They can stop trying to control each other. They can be adventurous with each other, since they feel secure in their own individuality that they have carefully nurtured, and respect the same in the other. They can intentionally pursue unique interests, engage in separate activities and consort with different friends. They understand that separating themselves in this fashion creates distance, and some tension. With the benefit of that distance they can behold the other almost as they did that first time, as a fresh partner. They must then work hard to impress each other, for neither takes their place for granted. What creates a healthy and mutually beneficial dynamic then is the efforts they make against the separateness to pull themselves back together. When they regard each other up close, it is with the recognition that while no one person can fulfil all their needs, still they appreciate all that the other offers.

Once they are close again, they must immediately be on the watch for signs of falling into old patterns of predictability that make things go stale. They must be willing to let each other go again, and embark on strong individual pursuits. This does not mean complete freedom to do whatever one wishes without regard for the other's preferences. Complete freedom implies a zero relationship. When his partner goes out of line beyond their accepted boundaries, whatever those may be, man must respectfully call her out, and he should be ready in turn to face her outrage if and when he transgresses. Both partners expect the other to call foul when they commit a foul, because only that demonstrates that they are not indifferent to each other. For the relationship to stay healthy, they must relate with intent from positions of individual strength. They are like two distinct stars in a binary constellation, forever balanced between coming together and flying apart.

Kindness towards the other, both felt and demonstrated as regular acts of kindness, is the key to sustaining a healthy relationship. Man often replaces his kindness with conditional acts seeking something in return, which the other party often recognizes and resents as a transaction intended to create an obligation to reciprocate. Or, he ignores his own boundaries and tries to appease his partner at all costs, by propitiating towards the partner as if he or she were a deity. This sort of appeasement encourages condescension towards the one who constantly bows his head. For kindness to be effectively received and go towards contributing to the overall health of the relationship, it must neither be transaction nor propitiation. On the other side of the equation, sustained acts of disrespect, and its accompanying end state emotion of contempt, are sure signs that the relationship is headed towards a separation or divorce. Once a state of contempt is reached, it is very hard to recover and put the relationship on its tracks again. Feelings of contempt makes man turn a blind eye to even genuine efforts at reconciliation from the object of contempt. Every act or utterance from the other, no matter how it is intended, is received with the same contempt.

These then are the salutary effects of healthy loving relationships on man. Can he have too much of a good thing? Is there such a thing as a limit to one's love? Can he love more than one, or have as many lovers as he can possibly fit into his life? He is tempted to say yes, of course. The flights of the mind do not take practical considerations into account. Even when he tries to apply reason, if one is good, more is better, man believes. Thinking along these lines, one or both partners can add others to the existing relationship, for sexual variety, for excitement, for love, or simply in recognition that any one individual cannot meet all of the other's needs. Under names such as polyamory, polygamy, open relationships, or other unnamed variations, man tries to maximize his relationships in an attempt to seek happiness.

Love

To the extent that all parties can stay somewhat satisfied and content, these arrangements may serve their purpose. All too often though, the same dynamics that apply to a relationship between two, apply in even more complicated fashion to a relationship between three or more. When man is with one partner in a triad, he is evidently not spending time with the other, and that is a conscious choice on his part that rankles the third who is left behind. Jealousy, attempts to control the other, practical considerations, constraints of time, money and logistics, all undermine the extra gains of happiness one seeks. Polyamory means multiple partners but also multiple problems with multiple dimensions. There is no free lunch to be had.

Love is a delicate plant, forever like a freshly planted sapling. It requires careful nurturing to flourish. When man the gardner is with the object of his love, he must regularly give his undivided, undiluted attention. There is a limit to how much time one has in this world, and this puts a practical limit on how many partners he can add without diluting the quality of the love. Fundamentally, one of the truest measures of love is the time one can commit this love, since that is the only commodity that is limited for everyone. It takes a special person to not feel slighted when the hours spent together diminish in favor of another lover. Many will respond with jealousy, or at least by proportionally scaling back the love they give in return. When man divides his love, the recipients of his fractional love also typically wish to give no more back in return than what little they recieve. Eventually, many of his secondary loves will drift away and lose touch with him. He is then back where he started.

Romantic partners, family, friends and pets are not the only loves of man, of course. He can and does express love for inanimate objects, and may vehemently insist that he loves them just as he might a human. He can love his car, his job, his co-workers, his gadgets, his wine or art collection, his lizard, his football team, his president, his nation, etcetera. His limbic brain tries to form bonds with everyone and everything in sight, other people of course, but also arbitrary things and loose collections of strangers who may not even be aware of his feelings. Alternatively, he may say that he loves nature, animals, humanity, or all of God's creations. Whether secular or religious in origin, this is an all-encompassing kind of love. He then takes joy in living a life of devotion to his loves, such as by serving the poor, taking care of orphans, running an animal shelter or being a caretaker for a forest. Unfortunately for him, these sorts of love are wholly one-sided. The objects of his love have no feelings, and therefore cannot reciprocate his devotion. He may indeed receive praise and recognition from others for his noble actions, but to derive true satisfaction for such kinds of love, he must hold no expectations of receiving anything in turn.

When man questions his purpose in life, how do the wise reply? When the soul is troubled, what do they say will save it? Love, comes back the whispered answer. Love is proclaimed as the magical balm to soothe all pain. Yet, for something that is so critical to his happiness, he has little control over it. Love for him thus hinges on the act of giving, not receiving. He cannot control being loved back. And what he mostly cannot control, he must mostly let go of. Love then is primarily a sacrifice that he makes while ignoring the demands of his own ego, that voice that demands reciprocal worship. Those he cares for may care for him in return, and yet there are no guarantees in love or life. Ultimately, he has one life to live. He can choose who to love and how to love. Then, he must confront the paradox that whether he finds love in return or not is dependent not on how hard he looks for it or how much he tries to secure it, but how strong he is to let the objects of his love roam free, and to roam himself.

Work

Love and work are the cornerstones of our humanness.

- Sigmund Freud

"He works seven days a week, nonstop. Normal for him is 80-90 hours, but there's times he pulls all-nighters and puts in 100+ hours. He's gone before the kids wake up and back only after they're asleep, so they're practically growing up without a dad. Then he comes to bed with that darn phone and sits up working till 2AM. We usually fall asleep like that. Sundays he tries to take a break, but he's so exhausted that he spends it sprawled out on the couch, bleary eyed and yawning, recovering from the week and getting ready for Monday. I know he loves me and the kids, and he feels guilty for not spending time. But if it's between us or work, he has to choose work."

- Wife of a worker

Man today lives in a culture of all-or-nothing work. Work culture regards human beings as automatons that must produce, and nothing more. Another way of saying this is that in this system, if one isn't a worker, one is nothing. He lives primarily to work, and the rest of his life revolves around subservience to the temple of work. Work gives him livelihood, purpose, and a means to fill every waking hour. In return, he must devote himself fully to this temple. It demands total dedication, no matter what. His only other choice is to do nothing, and be nothing - at least in the eyes of the believers. Freud's observation about love and work being the two foundations for man to be fulfilled did not account for a situation where he must constantly choose between the two.

There is little doubt that no other sphere of man's life gives him more purpose that his profession. Even when a man says that he hates his particular line of work, he values it far more than just the money that it brings in. After all, he is free to leave at any time. Work is employment at will, for both parties concerned. Yes, there may be bills and expenses to be paid, but he will keep working past those needs being met. Until the day that he quits, he derives meaning and satisfaction from it. Work provides him with opportunities to prove himself, to succeed at challenges and be recognized for the success, and a means to demonstrate his skill at leading others. He often grouses about the arbitrary nature of work and its various demands on his time and energy, but he complains only while safety entrenched in the job. From the perspective of the unemployed, who would gladly trade places with him, this reeks of a certain hypocrisy. Work is man's anchor, and an anchor is of no use without its heavy chains.

Society highly values the normal working man, the kind who goes about his job daily without complaint. Children are taught from an early age to think about their adult selves, and the question often posed to them is what they want to be when they grow up. Yet, when the child does grow up, he finds that work in the form of brutally long hours alienates him from the essence of human existence. All other spheres of life - time spent in play, in communion with friends or family, in creative acts, in recuperation, or simply in quiet solitude - must be deducted against time spent working. When work takes on an all or nothing quality, the available choices are to work intensely, or just step off the whole train altogether.

Work

A few men are all-in for work. This sort of man is a total worker, and little else. All his hopes and desires are stirred in the same pot as with his career goals. He has thrown his fate to the mercy and goodwill of his employers or business. He labors every waking hour of the day, save for breaks for eating, excreting, and maybe exercising. His entire existence revolves around work, and if one tries to take him away from his work for a moment, his thoughts are constantly returning towards what he wants to do next and whether he is being productive now. He feels constant guilt for not devoting even more time towards work. His life is optimized towards maximal work output, and every other thing is subservient to the God of Work. Such a man lives to work, and without it he is nothing. He hustles, round the clock.

Society rewards such men with titles, status, power, recognition and money. He works hard, they will say, and that one quality will excuse all other deficits in such a man. Since his happiness is tied intimately to his work, his moods will experience the ups and downs in accordance with the variance of sales figures, stock prices, valuations, performance evaluations, promotions, or whatever else that he has placed significance upon. When things are going well at work, he soars, and his star rises up, and he feels powerful and invincible. When things suffer, he feels embarrassed and diminished, he wants to hide, and he wants to escape. He may consequently suffer from spells of addiction, aggression, or depression, but work does not care. He must pull himself out from the depths and return to work each morning with fresh enthusiasm.

Primitive man derived direct and visible meaning from any work that he undertook, such that he would have no reason to even invent a word for it. If upon waking up he set a few snares for trapping small mammals, collected drinking water and dry wood for fire, felled trees to make a clearing for his new hut, built that hut, and stacked heavy rocks together for a hearth, he did all that because he needed to. If he didn't do it, there would be clear and easily understood consequences. There was no great struggle in understanding the point of stacking the rocks, because it was the difference between freezing miserably in the cold and enjoying a warm fireplace. The closely coupled nature of his work and its immediate impact on his world made it much easier for the primitive to do what was necessary, when it was necessary, no less, no more. In contrast, modern man's work is similar to that of a monkey in front of a contraption. He pushes the buttons because he knows he has to, but he cannot possibly understand all that's going on behind the scenes. He works as the tiniest of cogs for the most massive of corporations in an unfathomably complex world, talking airily about how he does this and he does that, while comprehending so little that it amounts to nothing.

Hard work isn't a new invention, however a feature of work today that did not exist before is its exhaustless and omnipresent nature. If there was a stand of trees to be felled, limbed, bucked into logs, split and stacked, then man could see the progress he made, and he did not carry the work with him wherever he went. In contrast, work today often does not follow these rules. It is inexhaustible, it does not show progress easily, and it follows him everywhere he goes. One can go home and continue to work, which is a boon for employers since they can call their hours flexible and yet extract maximum output. Indeed, if the employee can take pride in anything, it is in always being available. He rushes at all hours of the day to react to tasks before others notice his slightest delay, and in doing so he takes much pride.

Modern work is arbitrary in terms of the nature, timing and sheer quantity of the demands it places on man's thinking apparatus. All day, he receives urgent indications to perform a random series of tasks. These tasks are conveyed to him via instantaneous digital means. He cannot anticipate these demands, and rarely does he wake up with the knowledge of what is on his list of things to do. Nevertheless, it is his responsibility to see them to completion, without regard to personal affairs. He carries around at all times in his head maybe ten or twenty or even a hundred tasks that he has yet to do. Sometimes he attempts to write them all down so he won't forget, but there's too little time to even do that, and there's always more things coming. Naturally, he knows that he forgets a few things now and then, and this causes him great distress. He constantly fears that he is missing something important. He paces restlessly, he fidgets, and he endlessly checks his digital devices even when he is not at work, such that he is indeed always at work. He is overwhelmed by his daily burden. Like the drowning man who churns the water as he sinks into a bottomless lake, he thrashes wildly through his days at work.

Daily escapes for a man trapped in the temple of work include a mindless and hurried consumption of fast foods, caffeine and other stimulants, alcohol, and distraction via screens that deliver doses of social media, stocks, sports, news and entertainment. The latter distractions are available to the worker at the press of a button, precisely because he does not have much time to spare. The apps that deliver these are intricately designed by large teams of other workers to be optimized for quick and smooth consumption. They contain reinforcement mechanisms to train a worker to keep coming back for more. The gratification is instantaneous, cheap and plentiful, yet are never ultimately satisfying, which are perfect conditions to develop an addiction. Over time, the behavior of a worker in his cubicle, taking a break from work, looks no different from that of a pigeon in Skinner's Box, trained to peck for grains of food.

Ironically, a great avenue of escape for the all or nothing worker is work itself. He will first endure long hours at the office, to the point of near exhaustion. Then, in a brief moment of respite, such as when he relieves himself, his thoughts return to his condition. He is reminded of the barren nature of all the other spheres of his life that he has neglected in favor of work. Naturally, he finds these thoughts extremely distressing, and attempts to alleviate his mood. Since he was hard at work until a few moments ago, work is the nearest available distraction, and there is always plenty more to do, so he dives right back in. With his mind engrossed he can forget everything else. He continues like this late into the night until true exhaustion sets in. Then he can drop right into sleep for a few hours until the next day comes around, when he can repeat the cycle of workaholism anew.

After a few years of riding this wagon, man is tempted to jump off. He develops elaborate escape fantasies, which typically involve changing careers and perhaps changing locations too for an alternate lifestyle that buys him a sure ticket to a happier life. In most cases, the fantasies are just that. He doesn't know how to exit, and he is too busy to even take the first steps. Often, he is trapped in place by an intricate web of financial commitments built up over time that leave no room for change. In addition, he fears the loss to his identity if he makes a mistake and ends up in a less important role. Occasionally he does manage to change employers or locations to give himself a fresh start. The new profession invariably turns out to be not that different in terms of the demands it places. Of course, there are good times, when man feels energized and works hard to solve fresh challenges. More often than not though, the old pattern of destructive tendencies and depression returns, with added bitterness because now one has tried to change things and failed. His escape fantasies now morph into death wishes, since the only viable escape from it all is a permanent one. Sure enough, many highly stressed all-work professionals such as lawyers, doctors, and bankers exhibit high suicide rates.

Work

Other men have the flip side of the coin. They have chosen to check out from the culture of work. In reality, this isn't an active choice in most cases. In the highly mechanized and automated economy, there often isn't enough good work to go around. When there is work, it barely pays the bills even when one works long hours. Man can thus be fully employed and yet in poverty. He realizes that earning a full week at minimum wages leaves him with scarcely more money than if he had just sat around and collected unemployment benefits from the state. Still, hard work is a prized concept for the working class man. His culture tells him that he supposed to suck it up and shut up. Perhaps he keeps at it for a few more years, struggling to find gainful employment, bouncing from one option to another, before finally giving up in frustration. The rational non-skilled worker reaches a point of being indifferent to having or not having a job.

Enter part time work, gig work, shift labor, or all the other names that apply to the largest segment of the working population. Firms needing unskilled or semi-skilled labor lure him in with assurances of flexible hours and slightly higher than minimum wages. Sure enough, compared to a nine to five, the hours are adjustable. The conditions though are bleak, and the endless menial tasks slowly numb the mind and crush the soul. This work is conducted in vast warehouses, farms, factories, industrial kitchens, or delivery vans, out of sight or cut off from the ebb and flow of normal life. There is nothing lasting or significant that he gets out of the mechanical repetition of tasks, and he knows it. There are no co-workers to bond with, as everybody is a replaceable and frequently replaced cog in a giant machine. He responds by doing the bare minimum to get by. He earns what he needs to for food and rent, and little else.

Occasionally, he forsakes this kind of work completely and lives off his savings, off his parents or his partner, off benefits, off this and that. He calls himself alternative, non-corporate, and nobody's grunt, but yet he is a grunt. He is free, but of nothing in particular. Choosing to opt out of the pact of work comes at a heavy price. For having abandoned the working life, he misses out on all the perks and gifts lavished on those who are on the other side of the employment fence, but the loss goes much deeper beyond that. Hard work and the corresponding feeling of being useful as a provider is the fuel that sustains man's pride. Both genders suffer from being unemployed, but masculine identity is especially tied heavily to work. In a society that places high value on judging the character of man by his profession, having no work to report of leaves man without definition, without character. He feels judged by all as either lazy or useless. He lashes out in anger at those who he feels judge him. His relationships with mainstream society wither and suffer, and alongside diminishes his potential for lasting romantic relationships. When love and work are the cornerstones of man's humanness, if one of these two pillars are lost, the other soon collapses alongside.

Man once claimed honor in providing for his family, in being the bread-winner, in performing the modern equivalent of the heroic hunter bringing home a big hunk of meat. In today's world, he still craves the patriarchal entitlement of sitting back and relaxing at the end of the day and basking in his woman's loyalty and deference, but if he is unemployed, he has done nothing to earn it. He sulks and whines, and he does little to contribute to chores around the house. He feels wronged, first by his employer, then by society, and ultimately, by those around him. His outrage is felt by those closest to him. Alcohol, drugs and addictive painkillers now often take on roles as surrogate sources for happiness to be sought from, despite their destructive potential. Of course, not every man responds negatively or with resignation to the lack of gainful employment. Some will craft an alternate identity in being a good father or husband or son, in being helpful to those around him, in volunteering for his community, or in creating beautiful things of artistic or aesthetic value. The gap he seeks to fill in his life is large, and he must think big and act larger still as he crafts an alternate identity to replace that lost from lack of work.

Being unemployed or underemployed brings its own unique problem in terms of what to do to kill the hours of the day. Passing time is a primary preoccupation of unemployed youth around the world. In contrast to those who worship work, for whom time is a precious commodity, the slacker must find a cheap and effective way to relieve boredom on a daily basis. The global technology and entertainment industries are now heavily geared towards providing the means for large cadre of youth with a means of passing time smoothly. Their slacking off invariably happens with a screen, where several hours a day can be spent grazing and consuming a variety of videos, images, and games. This web addiction further isolates man from his surroundings and from others around him. It also effectively limits his chances of getting out of the situation he finds himself in.

The issue for young workers today is one of increasing purposelessness. As living standards rise across the globe, the basic necessities of life get easier to procure, while increasing automation shrinks jobs. Whether to embrace work or to opt out of it becomes an especially pertinent choice. For a youth from an impoverished family, the only question is how to rise up in the world and gain wealth. He may harbor a fire in his belly that drives him to seek a way out. He has no quandaries about embracing any ladder that takes him to the top, even if it is at the expense of his own wellbeing. He will gladly be fodder to a cult of work, and employers will love him for it. On the other hand, a young man of affluence may tend to reject the working life as one filled with mindless drudgery and boring conventionality. The irony is that it is his parents' participation in the workforce that allows him the financial security and the freedom to now reject it. His role models are the social media stars who flaunt various alternate and nomadic lifestyles as tempting examples to follow. If this lifestyle leads to a dead end in a decade or two, in terms of career progression, job stability, or building a family, that remains hidden until it is too late.

The question for the older worker is one of relevance. Staying relevant means feeling useful, being productive, and knowing that one's skills are valued. This is increasingly difficult as one ages, since faculties and capacities for pure output diminish with the years. The all-work economy values efficiency over all other traits. This naturally favors a younger worker, with his fresh eyes, quick hands, and big hunger. Information is increasingly systematized and written into software, such that the experience and knowledge that an older worker might possess is rendered irrelevant for modern processes. An older mechanic might know how to fix a faulty component, but the economics favor swapping out for new parts rather than repairing the old. In addition, the pace of change is relentless. This again favors younger workers, who are more flexible in adapting than those with crystallized ways. The older worker must therefore gravitate towards professions that take advantage of their greater life experience, so they can teach or mentor others, rather than focus on pure individual output.

In the end, man's satisfaction from work depends on the health of his relationship to it. His must not take it for granted, yet at the same time he cannot become so dependent on it to impart meaning to his life that he has no life left outside of it. If he acquires the education and the skills needed to climb out of the labor economy at a great expense, he may have to enter the temple of work crawling on all fours. Despite this prone stance with which he begins his career, he must find the internal resolve to stand up and reject the cult of work, at least for a few hours each day, to connect with his fellow humans outside of it. He must remember that anything that a man can do will one day eventually be done by a machine, and when those tides turn, the only professional traits left for humanity to value will be genuine human emotion, empathy and creativity. He thus has no choice but to also devote himself equally to his family, his arts and crafts, his passions, and his community. In doing so, he must have the courage to reject society's condemnation of his work-life choices. A society that worships at the temple of work forces man into one of two extremes, neither of which is fulfilling and contributes much to his happiness. Somewhere between the cult of work and the cult of the slacker, life can be found. It is up to man to stand up tall on this precarious rock and hold fast against the waves that seek to wash him off into the depths.

Play

The real secret to life is to be completely engaged in whatever you are doing in the here and the now... and realize that it is play.

- Alan Watts

"I play about 20 hours a day, most days, I guess..."

- South Korean teen at a gaming den.

What does man do, when he doesn't need to do anything at all? Say that he is well fed, rested, safe, comfortable, and all his bodily needs have been met for the moment. Consider the impulse that strikes man in such a state. Does he lie in passive enjoyment for more than a few moments? Usually, not for very long. His restless nature takes over and he gets up. He needs something to do. He tends to want to find something that distracts, and lose himself in either a creative act or a consumptive act. He wants to play.

Play is best described as activities that man willingly chooses to engage in, to occupy his mind with anything but empty thoughts, to bestow the hours of his days with importance, and to make him lose track of the passage of time. Work, whether in the form of earning a living or necessary household chores, does not meet this definition because it is not truly voluntarily chosen. If one is a believer, the obligation he feels to give service to a God, a church, a revolution, or a cause do not constitute play. The same applies to basic acts of maintenance and propagation such as sleep, sex, feeding himself, and taking care of himself and others around him, all of which he is somewhat obligated to do. Everything else is play. And the way in which he plays says a lot about him. One can learn more about someone by watching him play for an hour than a year's worth of conversation.

For man to persist with an act of play, it has to have the necessary component of engaging the mind and the senses. Anything that doesn't hold his attention is quickly discarded as boring, and he moves on something else. This wandering happens because once play stops engaging his mind, it frees up his thoughts. Those thoughts invariably come back to the one thing that is a constant in his life. Man never forgets his true condition. If he has a moment to himself without anything at all to do, that old realization rises up again. In response, he seamlessly and continually seeks out an endless series of diversions all day to escape the thoughts in his own head. At least when is hungry or hurting or cold, there is an immediate and real problem to be solved that takes his attention. In a way, having an immediate need to take care of, even if it is a small itch, is far better than the alternative of silence with one's own unbearable being.

Consequently, he has developed an infinite variety of ways in which to divert himself. He plays games, he plays sports, he watches screens, he listens to music, he reads, he writes, he walks, he runs, he studies, he goes on aimless drives, he browses stores, he shops, he collects things, he eats and drinks despite being not hungry, he gossips, he socializes, he kills time. He learns things, he designs and builds things, he destroys things. He goes to festivals, he visits amusement parks, he attends concerts, and he travels around the world, taking pictures of himself at the places he goes and the sights he sees. He cultivates a hundred hobbies and a thousand interests. All forming a grand and lifelong exercise in diversion.

Play comes in fundamentally three forms, with varying contributions to happiness. The first kind of play is spontaneous play, entered into simply for fun. This is play partaken with no goal or intent in mind. A child comes across a puddle after the rain and jumps and splashes. A group of teenage girls on a sleepover break into a pillow fight. A man and his dog chase madly after shorebirds on the beach. Two lovers entwined tumble on fresh snow in a mock fight. This is the kind of play entered without prior anticipation, and one does not reflect much upon it after it concludes. It is simply something that happens when it happens, if the conditions are right, and spontaneously, like spiraling leaves chasing after each other in a fall wind.

In the midst of this form of play, man loses himself totally. For a few moments, he forgets about himself, his troubles, his worries, and just plays. Children play in this manner all the time. They play for the sheer joy of it. Their developing minds lack yet a full conception of life and its limitations. Their play is not an attempt at distracting themselves from their concerns. Instead, the play itself is their concern. When man plays like that, he gets to be a child again. He separates himself from his normally constricting conception of self and just exists in the moment. He pauses being self-conscious and steps outside of his own mind. It is essential for the soul and spirit, for him to remember that he isn't just the view he sees from the inside. Spontaneous play does that for him.

The difference between man and child is evident though when play ends, as it inevitably must. The child may cry because he wants to keep playing. The man might not cry, but as the lingering excitement fades, he gets sombre in remembering everything once again, and gets all serious. He may even feel a bit embarrassed for getting carried away in such a childish manner. He looks around to make sure that nobody has witnessed his immaturity. Society conditions him to not be too playful, else he betray his lack of maturity as a grown up. As the child grows older, he learns to replace spontaneous acts of playing with rigid and planned play sessions. His parents and teachers encourage this structuring by providing him with games with set rules, fixed time slots for when he can play, formal coaching lessons, and other rigid frameworks.

This maturation culminates into the second kind of play, which is structured play. Adults typically play with a specific intent in mind. Maybe there is a specific time or place associated with it, there are complex rules, or one needs some special equipment or gear to play. In some way or another, this play isn't free form. Simply the fact of being a grown up bears down heavily on how play plays out. Adults cannot kick a ball around aimlessly for long without getting impatient about when the real play will start. Structured play does not lighten man's soul to the extent that the spontaneous kind can. It does however serve to develop his character, knowledge, and mastery of skills. Where previously there was no concept of winning or losing, no concept of getting better at something, no concept of dedicating oneself, now there is all that.

Structured play may not always be fun, at least in the moment to moment experience of it. Speaking a new language or learning to ride a unicycle can be difficult and frustrating. Having to interact with strangers to create a play or a production together can give rise to much discomfort and social anxiety. Traveling to explore new destinations requires much hassle and prior planning. Undertaking a long backcountry hike often means trudging over rough terrain in the heat or cold under heavy loads while enduring pain or discomfort. These sorts of activities are joyful in the sense of what man gets out of them later, retrospectively. This could be a sense of accomplishment, a feeling that he did something, that he learnt something new, that he experienced the world rather than merely surviving it. Any trouble that he endures is worth it because after completing the play, he   is better than before at whatever it is that he played. As his skill, knowledge or accomplishment improves over time, he can perform at a higher level, and look back at the progress he has made. This increases his satisfaction with his conception of himself. He is man, improved.

If there is a good match between man's interests and abilities, and the challenge that play presents, then he enters into a state called flow. In this state, he is fully engaged on the task at hand. He completely loses awareness of everything except the very thing he is focused on, as he concentrates on beating the challenge. He stops noticing sounds, sights, smells, events or people around him. Any number of activities can get man into a state of flow. When one is performing a song or dance on stage, that is flow. When one is competing in sports, whether against a human counterpart or just a stopwatch, that is flow. When one is engrossed in a complex puzzle where the solution always seems just out of reach, that is flow. When a pianist plays a challenging piece that he enjoys, that is flow. When one is rolling in a jiu-jitsu competition with an equally skilled opponent, that is flow. When one is skiing downhill as fast as one can while staying at the very edge of control, that is flow.

The great thing about flow is that it manages to keep man's interest for as long as he is willing or able to expend the effort. Of course, effort is never be limitless. Flow activities are energetically demanding. Sooner or later, he has to balance how much energy he spends in flow versus what he has left over for the rest of his life, namely work, chores, and family

Play

obligations. He must be careful not to carry them to an extreme. This is precisely the difference between enjoying a challenging sport, and becoming addicted to it to the point that one spends hours at it daily, neglecting all else. Nevertheless, the expenditure of effort required in attaining and sustaining flow is usually well worth it. The sweat that he must shed and the calluses that he must acquire give him a high to enjoy and savor long past the activity itself has ended.

Competition is a formalized way to engage in flow. As they say, all competition is a case of you versus you. Even as he faces other men, at the core of the matter, he is pushing against his own limits. Before the competition begins, he may make all sorts of excuses in his head, listing out all the things that aren't in his favor, and go over all the reasons why he shouldn't be competing at all. After all that doubt, when he finally competes, he diverts all his energy towards winning. There is a certain honesty that is attained. Either he wins or he loses, but he tried. This is why opponents will genuinely embrace each other after their battle ends. Irrespective of the results, they know where they stand. The self awareness that is gained from competing at peak flow results in a deeply improved man.

Exploration is a form of play that combines spontaneity and flow. Traveling to new places is the most common way in which man explores his world. When he travels, he is open to spontaneous experiences. Since he does not know what he may encounter, he must be on his toes and engage all his senses to deal with the new environment. Travel forces him to adapt to the world, instead of his usual mode of operation, which is trying to adapt the world to his needs. In this way, travel broadens his capabilities and perspectives. When he is roaming the villages and countrysides, soaking up urban life, or hiking deep into the wilderness, he steps out of his mind. He stops focusing on his troubles, and he lives in the present. This is that spontaneous flow state that man enjoys so thoroughly. Yet, for some, travel is simply a means of running away from one's present life. When taken to that extreme, travel becomes yet another form of escapism, and ultimately a futile one. He desperately takes the remotest roads into the farthest corners of the planet, as if trying to shake the demons on his tail, but the demons stay with him tight and inseparable as a shadow. Man can never run from himself.

The last kind of play that man engages in is when he seeks cheap distractions. This is play purely as a means of escape. Escapism via play can take many forms. Video games, movies, books, television, drugs, etcetera can all fill the role. What determines whether it is escapism or not isn't the activity itself, but man's relation to it. Play for escapism differs from other kinds of play in that it is typically an addictive, mindless activity that involves low effort and instant rewards. The most efficient avenue available to man today for comprehensive distraction is the internet, where he can rest his body in a vegetative state while his eyes graze over a landscape of billions of videos, images, and text. This is his ultimate affliction, representing all the progress he has made, and allowing him to spend nearly his entire lifetime in passive absorption of electronic stimuli. When man surfs the internet, he is simultaneously the creator God and the spellbound voyager in a spacecraft as he floats through a vast virtual universe of his own creation, where infinite galaxies invite his exploration.

This illustrates a key distinction between how play used to be and what it has evolved to be in the modern world. Thanks to the infinite stream of digital information that floods his senses, there are always more things to watch, more things to read, more things to hear, more ideas to follow up on, more games to play, more cool places to visit, and more exciting things to pursue. He fears that he is missing out on the fun if he doesn't do more. He tries to get to the bottom of his list, but of course the list is endless. He is a finite being, with finite time, energy and abilities, attempting to get through an infinite amount of play opportunities that are presented to him via digital means. Occasionally, with one eye nervously on the clock, he attempts to slog through his queue of unread books and unwatched movies and other such things he has saved for later, but this hardly succeeds any more than one can empty a river by drinking from it. He readily confesses that even when he tries to relax, it fails because he is multi-tasking and distracted. Activities that should be fun feel more like a chore than anything else. He then complains about being busier than ever, even though he is not busy working when he says this. In this strange way, his play now feels just like his job, except without the pay. The ultimate consequence of all this is that where play originally tended to be restorative for man, now it just overwhelms him and stresses him out.

At the other extreme, play becomes a mechanism not just to relieve boredom, but to relieve the fear of death. Whenever the experience of life starts to feel numb, man seeks to liven things up by applying to it deliberate brushes with death. He tries to walk closer to the edge with manufactured threats to his existence, such as rollercoaster rides, skydives, and bungee jumps, which supply him with mortal thrills in a safe environment. With repetition, these activities start to feel stale as the rush to the head fades, and so he then raises the stakes again with sports such as extreme downhill skiing, cave diving, or jumping off cliffs with a wingsuit. Other men choose more authentic and even higher probability threats to their own existence, such as racing cars at night with the headlights off, leaping off bridges into fast rivers, laying down on train tracks, pulling stunts with speeding motorbikes, playing with loaded guns, taunting policemen while armed, and shooting street drugs directly into their organs. For the thrill seeker, the appeal of these risks is simple. By showing a disdain for the dangerous consequences of his choice of activities, he seeks to take back control of his fate and mortality. The more he taunts death, the less he feels its grip on him.

Animals play too, but their play is mostly limited to the repertoire of skills they are born with. They can roll in a rough and tumble, they can wrestle, they can stalk and hunt, and they can chase tails, they can sing and call. They cannot play video games or watch reality shows. Animal play primarily serves to strengthen bonds between the playmates, including their human companions in they are pets. In juvenile animals, play develops the very skills that they will need later in real life. Some intelligent species of mammals such as dolphins and chimpanzees even appear to play out of sheer boredom. Still, although one cannot ask them this, it is unlikely that any animal plays as a form of escapism. No other creature resorts to play with quite the dedication that man applies to it.

Primitive man played too, but his play was limited by his technology. The human body of course formed the basis for many original forms of play, such as singing, dancing, play fighting, sports and games, grooming behaviors, running, jumping, climbing and other physical contests. He had weapons, hunting implements, crafts, plant and animal life, and the whole of the natural world to play within. Yet, when the body tires, the mind still needs diversions. Lacking the external technology to create inexhaustible diversions for himself, he instead turned to his imagination. The mind is a fertile factory for producing its own diversions. Magic, superstitions, rites, rituals, art, language, songs, stories, and symbolism, all originated from his prodigiously creative brain. Yet, the most engaging and rich form of play that he developed was conversation, especially the vigorous debates that were conducted nightly in public around the campfire.

Play

He began this play by categorizing everyone and everything that he encountered into opposing halves. Using just his wits, he made intricate delineations spanning the spirit world and the real world. Everything was labeled as either friend or foe, us or them, good or evil, living or dead, day or night, heaven or hell, sky or earth, barren or bountiful, and so forth. Then, he juxtaposed these forces against each other in a dynamic debate. Dividing everything into duals, debating their relative merits and worth, and moving them back and forth as opinions and facts changed, he was kept busy. Naturally, some of this play had a practical purpose. If he correctly categorized a stranger encountered when outside his tribe as friend or foe, then it aided his survival. Yet, survival concerns were a secondary benefit. The point was the play itself, because being good at it meant one knew what one was doing, which raised one's standing in the group. This play was always a matter conducted in public. What gave life to the play was to stand up and present one's ideas to the group, and to refute one's critics. It required much social delicacy to argue vigorously for one's opinions to gain consensus and become the group's opinions, while retaining the respect of the tribe and those whose opinions one had trampled over. This sort of play strengthened man's bonds to his tribe and simultaneously grew his brain power.

In contrast, man today often plays in isolation, and he rarely debates for fun. His choice of mental or physical activity is often solitary. Even when he engages in what he calls social media, he is isolated. He has a thousand friends, yet he is ever alone. He interacts with a screen alone, and the screen alone interacts back with him. His friend does the same, and yet the two do not ever connect or feel connected. The medium is the screen and the technology behind it. What it chooses to show him will always be self-limited and artificial, like the world of a fish staring at its reflection a fish bowl. All is good in this world. The water is always the same. The sights, sounds and textures are all uniformly comfortable and comfortingly familiar. Yet nothing is good in this world.

These are the ways in which man plays, and his motivations for play. As a spontaneous frolic in celebration of life, play can lighten the soul and lift his spirits. It can serve as an edge against which he sharpens his skills and strengthens his character. It can deepen his bonds with the fellow man with whom he shares play. Nevertheless, the primary purpose of most play as it exists today is to enable him to avoid honest thoughts of himself, his true condition, and his inherent loneliness. Terrified of finding himself alone with his thoughts, he chooses to sink into mindless diversions. For as long as he is able to sustain the diversion, he is dead to the world and the world is dead to him. This sadly becomes his happy state. Of course, he must exit the diversions at some point, and then he finds that he has successfully killed time without even being aware of its passage. He has lost yet another chunk of what precious life he has, and nothing was gained in the process. It is thus mindless play takes him deeper down into a pit of alienation and emptiness. All man needs to do to escape that pit is to play either in celebration of life or in pursuit of life skills, with his fellow humans as his able partners in play.

Virtue

"Bottomless pit of self-loathing..."

- Rock climber Alex Honnold on what drives him, prior
to his ropeless solo ascent of El Capitan

Whoever fights monsters risks becoming one. Gaze long
enough into an abyss, and it will gaze back into you.

- Friedrich Nietzsche

Whether he is bailing water while fighting to steer into big waves on day ninety five of crossing the Atlantic alone in a rowboat, or hallucinating while stumbling along lost and dehydrated in the dark fourteen hours into a hundred mile desert ultramarathon, or facing a wrist cramp after having climbed three thousand feet up without ropes on a sheer granite rock face, there is one thing about man's predicament in such situations that has a redeeming quality. At least in these moments of struggle, he isn't thinking about how his life has been a complete failure, simply because he never attempted to do something hard or very nearly impossible.

Man is engaged in a constant and pitched battle with the demons in his head. Their beastly voices murmur incessantly to him about his insignificance in this world. They whisper unpleasantly to him about his failings and worthlessness, and how the universe cares not one whit about who he is. Belittled in this manner, he feels driven to rise up and prove himself. He seeks to be the best he can be at something, anything. He wants to matter. He wants the world to notice him, and he wants the fellow man to respect him. He wants to do something nobody has ever done before, or do it as well as he absolutely can. He wants to possess virtue.

Virtue is the result of man's striving to rise above the ordinary. The word virtue here refers not to some goodliness or subjective positive quality in him, such as honesty, generosity or piety, but rather to his need to excel in his chosen dimensions, whether good or bad. A sprinter seeks virtue in running fast, a surgeon in operating flawlessly, a criminal in breaking the law magnificently without repercussions, and a serial killer in brutally murdering as many innocents as possible. The world has seen an equal share of good and evil deeds committed in the process of each man seeking his own personal brand of virtue.

As the accomplished climber Honnold admits, what drives man towards breathtaking feats is not so much the joy of succeeding, but rather the utter fear and loathing of ending up as what he considers a failure. The bigger the demons chasing after him, the faster he runs and the higher he climbs. The truly virtuous man doesn't simply want to be the best at his chosen field. Instead, he wants to be constantly improving upon himself. What he did yesterday was yesterday, it is today that matters. In this sense, as he seeks virtue, he is never satisfied with himself. He cannot look back upon how far he has climbed, because what matters is what lies ahead. Then when he surmounts a challenging goal, he finds no lasting joy in this success, except perhaps as a sense of relief as the tension and uncertainty dissipates.

Arete is another word for realized virtue. It is the result of sustained pursuit of mastery of a subject, of pushing constantly to improve, long past the point when the activity ceased to be merely fun, even to the point when any satisfaction derived from the act of striving itself is not enjoyable. Since true mastery implies perfection, and perfection is never achieved, arete requires one to stay at the edge of one's possibilities. The arete of a knife is to hold as sharp an edge as possible. The arete of a man is to operate at the edge of his capabilities in his chosen field. A man seeking arete is bound up in the act of living up to his full potential. This potential is an intrinsic value rather than an externally measured one. He cannot compare with the achievements of others, since arete is only attained in pushing one's own limits. If he does compare, he measures only against those superior to himself, to gauge just how far he has to go.

Arete is acquired by practice with intent. It requires training diligently while in flow states, such that all of his senses are fully engaged at a task. This is the situation of the tightrope walker traversing two buildings without a safety net, where one mistake means certain death. He has no option but to pay attention to what he does with every element of his being. When one stays on the edge, one gets sharper. Simply existing in a random collection of flow state however doesn't necessarily lead to arete. What matters is whether the improvements accumulate along the chosen dimension. The nihonto Japanese swordsmith folded the blade's iron upon itself several times to purify it, building up the homogenous grain alignment that gave the sword edge its great strength. Yet, if he made one wrong fold in an incorrect configuration, the strength advantage was lost. Similarly, man must stack his training purposefully in order to achieve arete.

In contrast to training purposefully to achieve arete, the time for chaotic, undirected play is early on, when he is still exploring his craft and choosing between his options. Children benefit from exposure to a variety of skills, games, sports and studies, because they are still forming the connections between their interests and their strengths. Playful exploration in childhood, youth and even into middle age is essential for man to find his unique brand of virtue. An apprentice bladesmith may indeed forge swords in all manner of right or wrong ways, because that is how he will learn, both from his mistakes and by discovering things that the experts missed. He may even abandon the craft and try out something else. However, when play ends and he seeks to improve, he has no option but to apply himself with all his being.

Some men are burdened with a great sense of loathing for their own inadequacy, and strive proportionally hard. They are constantly unhappy with their place in life, and seek to climb up endlessly. Many accomplished artists, athletes, entrepreneurs, etcetera suffer from this condition, to the extent that other men looking in might wonder why they are so dissatisfied with themselves despite their great life accomplishments. They do not realize that these achievers rely on that great unrest to accomplish those great feats. Seeking out great accomplishments as a source of life satisfaction presumes that one can accomplish much without being an inherently dissatisfied person in first place. Man cannot achieve greatness unless he suffers proportionally.

Success can come with or without virtue. The winds that govern man's fate when he floats adrift do not care about his virtue. The resolutely virtuous man knows this, and thus he is indifferent to success except as an external means of validating his arete. His success can indeed be aided by virtue, but it can just as often be a random fate of luck. As they say, it matters a lot to be at the right place at the right time. Success of this sort is like being carried forward at the crest of a wave that he happened to catch. He can be born into a family with the right conditions or connections. He could be born into wealth and influence that automatically translates into success. Virtue is not something man is born with, but rather a quality that he must earn by constant application to his chosen area. Measuring his virtue using his success as the metric is like attempting to judge the depth of a lake from the size of the ripples on the surface.

When success is easily acquired or inherited rather than earned, its provenance does not rest easy with man. He knows he doesn't deserve full credit for what he has accomplished, and this drives him to prove himself further. This is the sort of notion that grips the sons of millionaires, who desperately want to become billionaires, as if they can wipe the slate clean on their privileged background and claim virtue afresh. Alternatively, a man born to a highly accomplished family may choose to switch fields radically. He chooses a profession that flies in the face of all the plans, expectations and ambitions that his parents may have held for him. He does this so he can avoid an unfavorable comparison with his father and forefathers. Failing this too, he may reject all attempts at success, and plunge prominently deep into a life of wanton excess and carefully cultivated purposelessness. He plays a game of his own devising, and refuses to play the ones he can't win at. If it is well known to all that he does not care to accomplish anything, then he cannot be accused of being a failure.

Past successes do not improve man's satisfaction with the present. Success attained early in life does not carry forward as proportionate happiness later in life. The mere memory of success alone is no help. On the contrary, early success can work against future happiness, by leaving him with the feeling that all of his worth is spent, that his good days are behind him, and that he is no longer useful or capable of great things. He wishes to be forever productive. Typically though, his faculties and capabilities wane with time and old age. His performance suffers in absolute terms. His cherished run times, swim times, maximal lifts, and other personal bests will all fade away as increasingly distant and unattainable targets. Yet, the urge to excel does not wane with age. The drive to matter, to do something great, remains just as strong until one's last days. The urge may even get stronger, as he bristles against the limits imposed by his weakening flesh and society's condescension towards the old.

Success often visits upon the very young. Modern commerce favors profiteering from talent at any age. There are no minimum age limits to achieve success. The consumers of pop culture are ever younger, since they have an increased ability to spend and thus attract the attention of companies that have something to sell to them. The market craves youthful traits in performing artists, which drives ever younger stars to rise to the top. Athletes begin their training before they are done growing, and their peak performance comes even before they mature as an individual. Coders can release their software into the market and make millions while still not being old enough to drive. Naturally, many of these early successes will not repeat. A waning of abilities hurts far more than a low ability that holds steady or trends up. Professional athletes who are in their retirement, supermodels whose beauty has faded, child actors who failed to make it big as adults, or entrepreneurs who struggle to replicate the boom of their first startup, all suffer from comparison to their own pasts. The contrast hurts. Unhappiness to the point of suicide is rife in those who can't match their own glorious pasts. The higher one climbs, the further one can fall.

The oldest and most original kinds of virtue that man sought were of the physical sort. Before he evolved into the thinking animal, he was simply the animal. His body is at once the most impressive and accessible device at his disposal. His heart and lungs crave activity, his limbs love to flail, and his blood likes to pump. He continually strives to improve his body in both form and function. His flesh is the temple where he prays daily. The primitive must have sought and valued this virtue deeply, for how it translated directly into an easier existence. When the primitive child became a youth, he may have revelled in his vital physicality as he dashed full tilt through thick woods, as he swam effortlessly in water that was nearly ice, as he lifted and tossed around huge rocks, as he felled the largest of trees in a forest, as he subdued big prey or his enemies. He may have thought that it would only be the natural course of events for him to keep growing faster and stronger without bounds, until he could chase down antelopes and smash rocks with his bare fists. Throughout history, youth in their prime have had a tendency to fall into genuinely believing themselves to be nearly indestructible and practically invincible.

Man today spends an inordinate amount of time and energy on enhancing his fitness. He may focus on strength, speed, agility, power, endurance, flexibility, or some specific athletic performance. So he goes to gyms, he plays sports, he runs, swims, bikes, hikes and climbs, desperately seeking to mould his body along desired lines. When limited by biology or effort, he may even work on appearances alone, prioritizing form over function. He obsesses over the shape, bulk, and proportions of his body. In the opinion of some, this is a guiltless virtue, since nobody can be blamed for trying to improve upon the material and scaffolding of one's own construction. In the opinion of others, this is the ultimate in selfish and unproductive pursuits. No matter what he does though, the ravages of time reverse his progress over the decades. Aging inevitably deteriorates both his hard-earned fitness and his pristine looks, and reminds man of the folly of looking for happiness in some attribute of a perishable body. The only true satisfaction man can derive is in his stubborn belief in mind over matter, and his personal resolve to keep moving and keep lifting things despite the aches and pains, right up until that second when he cannot move a finger or lift an eyelid anymore.

For the primitive, although the desire to acquire virtue would have been just as strong, it was limited in scale. His arena was nature, and his energy was limited to what was contained in his body. He lacked the tools, machinery, devices and technology that man today employs. He lacked access to the nearly limitless energy from coal and petroleum that magnify his striving today. Modern life provides man with infinite means of distinguishing himself. The profusion of ways in which man expresses his unique virtue reflects his desire to stand out, like individual species in a rainforest ecosystem occupying different niches in order to flourish. He specializes in his own highly peculiar field to narrow the competition. He is one of the roughly only three hundred certified Tiffany lamp restorers in the world. He is one of maybe two dozen experts who truly understand the full scope of the threat of global nuclear armageddon. He is one of maybe five oncologists worldwide who specialize in treating mouth cancers in miniature pet donkeys. He is the sole researcher to have studied the mating behavior of a tiny tree frog that is only found on a small grove of trees in a remote corner of the Amazon. Culture is the end result of this endless drive towards specialization.

The pursuit of a unique brand of virtue is attractive especially because it allows man to escape the rigid confines of societal expectations. He can find relief behind new and constructed identities, which are free from the burdens of tradition. He has the freedom to create new looks, identities, sexual orientations, genders, professions and ways of living. For instance, a young male who is uncomfortable with patriarchal rituals and conventional displays of macho behavior, such as a pursuit of sports, cars, and girls, can reject those rigid norms by adopting a more gender neutral persona. He can take on any number of a variety of assumed forms. The risk that man faces here is that elaborately constructed identities can also serve as a mask to wear at all times, to avoid a painful confrontation of his realities.

Virtue

He might then exist as a shell around his core, emptied of any substance except the superficialities.

To avoid being stampeded and trampled over by the masses, man is desperate to stand out from the rest. And desperate men do desperate things. Nietzsche's caution applies strongly to he who seeks great virtue, especially if this a virtue along a self-centered dimension. The more deeply he engages in battle with his personal demons, the more selfish and ruthless he becomes in the process. He becomes a demon himself. Behind him, he leaves a trail of failed relationships, broken families, abandoned children, disappointed friends, and all those hurt when he ran over them in his mad dash towards a personal glory. He cannot relate to the world and to another human being without accounting for his own virtue agenda. Here lies the cause for a vast majority of the misery that man suffers and that he inflicts upon those around them.

Virtue can of course be of the subjectively positive, virtuous sort. This is where charity comes in. Charity is a voluntary act that benefits someone in need, typically with gifts of money. The popular meaning of virtue is associated with such acts of goodness. They say that man is virtuous when he is generous, when he is fair, or when he is kind. Generosity, fairness and kindness are admirable traits of course. Can man derive satisfaction from being virtuous in this fashion? The truth of the matter is that if he is mainly seeking external validation for his charitable displays, he is bound to be disappointed. Like the politician who attempts to win votes with his public works, all such a man is doing is trading his virtue for the praise of others. He does a mental accounting of what he has done and what he thinks he deserves, and if he fails to get the recognition that he thinks he deserves, he gets frustrated. Indeed, the vast majority of charitable organizations that exist today, exist to garner recognition for the wealthy donor, while helping him save on taxes. There is no true satisfaction to be had in living like this, always hungry for applause.

Then how about if man still does much good, but cares not for what the world thinks of him. Can he take a measure of internal satisfaction in bettering the world? Does the anonymous donor feel happy when he drops a bundle of bills into the donation box of a local shelter? Once again, it all depends on his motives. Such an act may just be contributing to a self-righteous adjustment of one's perception of oneself as a good person. A circular trade is at play here, since the person giving praise is the same as the person receiving it. He cannot fool himself into being happier simply by acting as a good person, if he doesn't attach an even deeper meaning to his actions. The best course is to be a virtuous individual not because of any praise or pride that he seeks to derive, but rather because he finds it truly meaningful to improve his world. The donor should take heed that charity that is undertaken simply to make the recipient happier has a better chance of making the donor happy as well.

Every man thinks that he is pursues virtue of a positive sort, irrespective of what dimension he has chosen to pour his energies into. He righteously believes that he is allied with the forces of fairness and justice, and that the path that he walks represents the carefully considered balance between his inherent goodness and some unavoidable acts of evil. All the murderers, despots, and genocidal monsters that this world has seen believe the same about themselves. None considers himself as pure evil. Even if his actions on the whole are universally condemned as evil, he truly believes he is the victim of his circumstances. He is totally consumed in fighting a pitched fight with his demons in the battlefield of his mind, but the carnage spills over into the real world in the form of his deeds. That he does great harm to the outside world is but unavoidable collateral damage in his epic struggle to push the limits of his existence.

Virtue

The obsessive pursuit of some personal virtue blinds man to the needs of others and binds him in a selfish web of his own creation. At the other extreme, he can also be guilty of curtailing all of his ambition and wasting his potential, simply because he prefers to avoid disappointment. When he tries and fails, the same demons rear their head up and relish in reminding him of how he was always bound to fail, and how everyone will now and forever judge him for his failure. Where he had wanted to stand out in success, instead he now risks sticking out even more prominently in failure. He wanted to dream of virtue, but he is afraid of not living up to his own expectations.

This is man's fear of dreaming. It is his oldest fear. From that distant eon, way back in time, when his primeval ancestors first crawled out of their murky ocean world to slither up the gravel beach. A fire in their bellies drove them to rise up from the dark depths and colonize land. Later, the same kind of dream drove the creature to climb down from the trees and start walking upright, to conquer fire, and to start hunting large prey. None of this was without risk. Yet, nobody that played it completely safe survived for very long on a geological scale. All men are descendants of those who pushed the edge, and yet somehow survived. Of course there were countless numbers who perished, and that fate strikes fear in those that remain. If man tries, he may certainly fail, but unless he tries, he cannot succeed. A satisfied life demands that he tries, and furthermore that he place no importance on the resulting success or failure. Dream on he must, for it is his inheritance.

Belief

I believe in my faith as I believe that the sun has risen: not only because I see it, but because by its light I see everything else too.

- C. S. Lewis

Isn't it just enough to see that a garden is beautiful without having to believe that there are fairies at the bottom of it too?

- Douglas Adams

The most notable thing that separates animal behavior from human is that animals do not believe in supernatural forces, causes, or higher powers. Animals are not activists, they do not join cults or fan clubs, and they do not pray. Man, on the other hand, is programmed to believe in something larger than himself. Belief is his acceptance that something exists or is true that transcends his own direct experience. He does not undertake this act of acceptance while standing on top of another greater truth. If such a greater truth existed, that itself would be the basis of his belief system, rather than the lesser truth that derives from it. His belief relies on its own merits, is self-contained, and impervious to external reasoning. His belief cannot be proven or disproven, or it would simply be a matter in the realm of science or experimentation. His belief is a leap of faith. He just believes in his belief.

Belief

Every child believes rather effortlessly. Children are fervent believers, in everything from fairies and ghosts to donkeys that talk and carpets that fly. Children are generally open-minded and unsuspecting creatures. They treat the world as a blank slate, as a book of rules that is still being written. They do attempt to seek cause and effect whenever possible, by asking a bunch of nested why-why-why questions. Still, they typically cannot yet apply skepticism given their limited supply of facts about the world. They may ask why the sky is blue, and accept that it is so because some giant being dipped his paintbrush into the azure oceans and then rendered the heavens. All of a child's initial causal beliefs come from parents, teachers and friends. Evolution safeguards the innocent child by having him follow unquestioningly at first, and only later develop reasoning and challenge the beliefs. Not surprisingly, the best way for any sect to grow the numbers in their congregation is to start recruiting its adherents from a very early age.

Once man starts down the road with his one fundamental assumption that cannot be proven, and that is his faith or belief, everything else that follows may indeed be logically sound. Entire edifices can now be constructed in great detail that stand on this one starting assumption that is the foundation of belief. Once the Egyptians had imbibed a belief in the afterlife and the status of their Pharaohs as intermediaries between the Gods and the people, what followed thereafter, such as conscripting tens of thousands of peasants over many decades to drag huge blocks of granite and limestone and build giant, pyramidal afterlife homes for the mummified remains of their pharaohs, all seemed justified as a logical next step.

With belief as his strong and immovable framework, man can now reason backwards from everything he sees in the world to prove his starting assumption, as if it were never an assumption at all. He sees the world as reflecting what is inside his head, and what he believes is indeed what he sees. The circle is complete, and order is restored to a chaotic world. His belief systems become frameworks that explain his actions and his world, and put them in coherent light. With belief as the principle, he need not worry so much about why he must do certain things and why the world works in certain ways. His mind is calmed immeasurably by the consonance and harmony he finds by residing in his faith-based framework.

Religion is of course the most timeworn and popular such framework, and not coincidentally, it is exceedingly cohesive at all levels, and comprehensive in its reach. Religion refers to a system of rules and powers that exceed human abilities. Faith is this religious belief acted upon, such that one places complete trust in God. Religious faith relies on bedrock that nothing is a true coincidence, that God's hand is behind everything that happens, from the gentle drift of a leaf falling to the ground to the motion of the planets and the stars themselves. It gives man coherence at all levels, small to large, personal to societal to global. Religion provides an explanation for all of man's questions and concerns, large and small, from birth till death and beyond even. It explains everything under the sun, it spans the entire universe and its creation, and it explains man's place in it.

Depending on the tradition, there may be some variances, but often the observance of religious faith converges to similar concepts. These concepts are along the lines of worship to God, service to others, acts of kindness, observance of rituals, restrictions and prohibitions on one's diet, sexual practices and other behavior, and paying monetary dues or offering one's labor to community building. The broad span of religion on one's life creates an immersive experience. It is an experience akin to mild hypnosis, and indeed many religious folk report trance-like states in the midst of their divine fervor. Affirmation of one's

Belief

faith and total submission to the omnipotence of God is a form of acceptance that relaxes and relieves man from carrying the burden of anxiety for his worldly affairs. The resulting reduction in stress has salutary effects even for man's health and wellbeing, such as for greater pain tolerance, and better remission rates, and improved prognosis for recovery from disease.

Religion may be the original belief system, but its ancient roots wrap around artifacts that modern man often cannot easily reconcile with his status as an enlightened and sophisticated being. Science is dispassionate and yet unrelenting in its attacks at the myths and miracles of religious faith. When man can step on a metal, plastic and sand contraption of his own creation and blast off to the moon and beyond, he can no longer look at the skies with the same wonder as the primitive who feared the comets as omens and lightning as God's wrath. Fortunately for modern man, he is equally adept at inventing other systems of believe in, to take the place of religion or to bloom alongside it. Despite what he might think, even the most secular and logical man believes in something. He may believe in the primacy of science or philosophy, for instance. Science was the first modern religion, but today he especially places his faith in technology, and on the continual march of technological progress.

Culture provides numerous other means of splitting mankind along two sides of a fence. He can be a conservative or a liberal, a patriot or a rebel. He can be an activist or an anarchist. He may be a diehard supporter of a sports team or a mad fan of some celebrity. He may be a sectarian who believes that his cult alone will survive doomsday, he may be a worker who believes that his startup will change the world, or he may be an environmentalist who believes that his actions will save the planet. Man can and does pull up all manner of factually true arguments to back up his belief. Nevertheless, when the belief system subsumes his personality, governs his actions, and becomes one with his worldview, he is no longer making an objective statement of facts but instead expressing his belief.

Mankind is split eternally between believers and non-believers. It could be that one man believes in a different system than the other, as in when he adheres to a different faith. It could be that he is an atheist, who is firm in his conviction that the belief is based on wrong, non-existent, or unprovable grounds. Finally, it could be that he is an agnostic, who recognizes that the faith in question is based on an assumption that can neither be proven nor disproven, and therefore accordingly refuses to believe or disbelieve. From the perspective of the believer though, a non-believer is a non-believer no matter what be his reasons. He may claim that even the non-believers do have a belief that they hold on to, in the sense that their non-belief orbits around a center of nothingness or a rejection of faith based systems. Irrespective, the believer cannot meet eye to eye with the non-believer. Either one has faith or one doesn't, and no amount of careful reasoning will convince one of the validity of the other's arguments.

Hence originates one of the great sources of evil for man. His belief gives him so much purpose and cohesion, that he may at times be willing to die for the sake of defending or propagating his belief. Along comes a man who questions his faith, and he is instantly a potential enemy. The stronger man's belief is, and the more extreme is his reliance on that system for his own comfort and wellbeing, the more threatened he is by an opposing belief. How he reacts now is also dependent on his belief. If the belief allows for coexistence with non-believers, then nothing need be done. If, on the other hand, the belief is silent about the possibility of other beliefs or even actively despises non-believers, the believer feels that he must act. This gives rise to the classic extremist, who will kill and destroy in the name of his belief. Since his belief system is so wonderful at explaining everything, all manner of actions can be justified in the name of his faith. All is fair and acceptable when one is on a crusade.

The self reinforcing nature of belief is such that unless the man is a rare skeptic, even direct observation of contradictory facts do not change the fundamentals of his beliefs. The conservative who views everything a liberal does as sinful, the liberal who believes everything about a conservative is evil, the arguing couple who each see everything the other person does as designed to hurt them, the madman who believes that everybody except he himself is insane, the conspiracy theorist who believes that everybody on the street is a government spy sent after him, they will all find ways to twist the interpretation of the facts to serve the needs of their belief system. At times, this requires much mental contortion and effort, as in the case of the Jonestown massacre victims who witnessed, allowed and even aided in the suffering, beatings, and eventual death by forced suicide of their own family members. When the core assumption that is a man's belief gives him such great mental comfort and coherence, it must remain unaltered, safe, and protected from the truth at all costs.

All belief systems are a great savoir to mankind when he feels troubled. As they say though, in order to be saved, one must first be lost. The Pirahã indigenous Indians of the Amazon resisted the missionary efforts to convert them because of their stubborn reliance on absolute truth. Their culture reflected a strong preference for living in the moment, right here, right now. Their language does not permit talk about events that have not been directly witnessed or heard from a direct witness. The absence of stories and myths in their world means that they are not easily persuaded to believe. In contrast, modern man is overwhelmingly surrounded by third party sources of information. He directly witnesses and experiences a much smaller fraction of his world than what he is exposed to indirectly, primarily via his consumption of digital and print content, books and magazines, the internet, and social media. If such a man needs to be sold on some belief system, it becomes a simple matter of first bombarding him with mass produced visuals, facts and stories that challenge his existing beliefs, such that he is left in a troubled state, adrift without anchor and clutching for solid ground. Then, when he is sufficiently troubled, when he feels lost, he can be saved by an alternate belief system that solves all the troubling questions and puts his mind to rest once again.

This is the organizing principle behind many of man's common beliefs. Once he has been made to worry that his heart will stop from consuming too much fat, he can believe that his brand of breakfast cereal will save him. Once he is made to feel insecure about his attractiveness, he can find respite by adopting clothes and gear that claim to give him a fashionable edge. Once he feels guilt and panic over the destruction of natural habitats, he can be made to believe that by buying more stuff made from organic and sustainable materials he can actually save the planet. Once he has been made to fear men from other races or creeds, he can be sold on a philosophy of arming oneself and closing up borders and minds. Once he is convinced that Armageddon is near and all except the believers will go straight to hell, he will tolerate and perpetuate hell on earth just to save himself.

Man is particularly attracted to belief systems that allow him to feel somehow more moral or pure than his fellow human. Not surprisingly, all religions have traditionally placed great importance on rituals that purify and cleanse, such as actual or symbolic washings, anointing with holy waters, burning to release fragrant smoke, or adorning with rosaries and garlands. They prescribe detailed practices and restrictions to keep the divine and the holy from commingling from the irreverent and the unholy, such as wearing certain garments at certain times, keeping certain foods separate from others, and segregating people based on their caste and implied divinity. Throughout history, the untouchables, the lepers, the menstruating, the irreverent, and the non-believers have all been lumped together as those to be avoided contact with. In the mind of the righteous believer, all earthly things must be forsaken as he seeks higher moral ground, in his endless pursuit to be more in touch with divinity, and to become divine himself.

Primitive man was an ardent believer. The earliest of ancient civilizations worshipped anthropomorphic figurines that symbolized fertility, virility, or shamanic power. They also created zoomorphic representations of animals that they feared, such as tigers and snakes, or animals that they depended upon for their survival, such as dogs, and later, domesticated animals. As civilization and its needs grew more sophisticated, the need for various Gods to worship increased in proportion, and they all needed distinct representations, for instance to distinguish the Rain God from the Harvest God from the Forest God. The worship of these various false idols, such as a statue, a picture, or a person in place of God, is now criticized by the sophisticated believer as a primitive practice. The traditional devotee is accused of confusing the symbols and representations of God with God itself. Of course, today one can find even more sophisticated believers, who claim that God itself is but a symbol of divinity or spirituality, and true belief should not make reference to any named God. This spiritual believer still believes, but in nothing but an unnamed, undefined entity. He has purified his belief to the ultimate degree, such that all that remains are the principles of divinity without any of the antiquated symbols. That way, he cannot be accused to subscribing to ancient, outdated belief systems. The driving principle remains unchanged, however. With every new evolution of belief, man seeks to find higher moral ground and attain a more pure form of divinity than the other believers.

Rational men tend to look down upon faith, especially belief in a God or higher power, as irrational. Such individuals, typically men of science and learning, were rare in primitive times but are increasingly common in today's world. They point to all the technological progress made by civilization and the material benefits brought about by their adherence to rationality as proof of its superiority as a framework. However, when these same rational men try to explain life itself in rational terms, they fail miserably. Life is undoubtedly absurd, and one cannot ever find logical grounds that can justify existence in the face of suffering. It is perhaps for this reason that the more educated and rational one claims to be, the unhappier he gets. He can simply never find peace in his mind, no matter how comfortable life gets. In contrast, the pious believer always has a means of explaining his life, as an existence in service to God. No matter how he may suffer, his mind enjoys greater peace.

The answer to the question then of whether faith heals man's pain, at least for the believer, is an unequivocal yes. If the belief system is comprehensive enough to span all levels from the minutiae of daily moments to the big questions about existence, then it calms his mind and secures his place in the universe. Religious faith is one such glue that binds man to all of his spheres in life, and gives him clear purpose for what he does and what he must do. Faith connects the finite existence of man to the infinite realms of time and space. The healing effect of faith is not just on the mind, because once the mind is healed, so can his body. Those who possess faith can truly be called the blessed, the fortunate ones, and their good fortune is precisely the fact that they have been saved by their faith. The challenge for man is that he cannot choose in his decision to believe. Either he has faith or he doesn't. Belief cannot be deduced or acquired from logical reasoning. On the flip side though, belief can certainly be undone if he desires cold hard logic in support of the core fundamental assumptions. And if what he observes

Belief

about the world around him does not supply such logic, he may well abandon the belief. His bold move comes at a heavy price, and the price is that he has lost the bedrock that had previously supported everything. Man then stands alone on the shores of a dark swelling ocean of uncertainty, and gazes fervently into the horizon in his search for meaning.

Meaning

Everything can be taken from a man but one thing: the last of the human freedoms—to choose one's attitude in any given set of circumstances.

- Viktor E Frankl

Our life is the creation of our minds.

- The Buddha

There comes a point in every man's life, when he has fought his battles and won some and lost some and yet more skirmishes loom ahead, if this man were to find himself standing alone at the edge of a cliff or an ocean, where he knows the wind or the waves or the vastness will swallow his voice unheard, and where there is nobody who will listen and nobody who will judge, to finally give in to the wild urge that arises unchecked now from the prior suppressed depths of his soul and compels him to open his mouth, take in a huge breath, and just scream.

Emptiness, alienation and boredom are the chief preoccupations of man today. Masses of humanity have arisen above poverty and enjoy ready access to food, water, shelter, electricity, sanitation, transportation, information at their fingertips, life saving technologies and medicines, and a variety of fantastical time-saving gadgets and entertainment options. By all measures, he should be in a state of peaceful contentment with his lot. Yet,

Meaning

these same masses spend their entire lives feeling dissatisfied. Men search desperately for someone or something to guide them, to show them the way, and to answer the question of what they should do with their lives. What's the point of it all, they ask, without ever receiving a satisfactory reply. Feelings of purposelessness has reached epidemic proportions in global society. Their lives, in their own words, are meaningless. And feeling this way can certainly detract from happiness.

Yet, a meaningful life is not the same as a happy life. One can perform a computation at any instant of a man's life, and say that a happy life is one where the past is filled with fond memories of joyful times, the present moment is packed with enjoyment of hedonic pleasures, and the future is brimming with optimism and a strong positive outlook. Defined in this manner, a happy life would also imply a life with a minimum of needless suffering. Imagine a fawn raised from birth in a large expanse of meadow. Plentiful lush green grass grows everywhere, fresh water runs in streams year round, and the land is free from all manner of pests and predators. Day after day, the fawn leaps and frolics in carefree and blissful divertissement with its herd of playmates, and grows up to be a handsome, well adjusted and sprightly young deer, until the moment that a clear head shot from the estate's gamekeeper lays it unceremoniously, unexpectedly, and instantaneously dead.

That was no doubt a very happy life that the deer enjoyed, by deer standards. Yet, most men would hesitate to trade places with it. Something about the pointlessness of its existence repels man. Of course, if he were that deer, he would not care nor know about such a thing as a pointless existence, but that is besides the point here. Man, the animal most deeply conscious of his own sense of self, is cursed with a need for deeper reasons to be alive that just surviving and thriving. He craves meaning. A meaningful life is a life imbued with a deeper purpose than mere superficial enjoyment of pleasures or minimization of suffering. A meaningful life is one where he does not have to stretch and reach and contort inside his head in order to justify his continued presence in the world.

Primitive man was forever ensconced in the rites and rituals of tribal life. In this he had no choice, obviously. Survival outside the confines of the tribe did not exist as a concept. He divided his world into competing duals, the good spirits and the evil ones, the living and the dead, the friends and the foes. The shamans were his guides for the spirit world and the real world, and any questions about the meaning of this and that were explained by a rich oral history of origin myths. Critically, he found no lack of purpose in his daily routine. Whether he gathered firewood to feed the campfire or took down an antelope to feed the tribe, he could explain and justify his actions with ease. Man as a primitive had no need to ruminate about the point of spending much of his time earning money that he does not have time to enjoy.

And then, in a blink of historic time, he pulled back from the warmth of the tribal campfire and instead leapt headfirst into the industrial furnace of modernity. The advent of civilization and early farming settlements delivered the first blow. He suffered from a loss of meaning, from having displaced the spirit world, the natural world, the shamans, the village elders, and the tribe itself. Later, he disbanded the large family unit, drove off the chieftains, and beheaded the kings. Over the last century, he unseated the priests and most of the ancient Gods from their high pedestals. In a few turbulent decades, he subsequently lost faith in all forms of government, nation, and polity as well. His final move is to increasingly abandon the institution of marriage, and with this last act he peels himself away from the embrace of the intimate family to stand all alone.

Meaning

With all the structure in his life eroded away, he sticks out, exposed to the elements. He gazes over the barren and ravaged terrain of his life and ponders what he should do next. What he ought to be doing is left undefined, for there is no one he listens to or can listen to now. In the vacuum left by the absence of higher authority figures, an anonymous, shapeless entity watches over him, his own guilt perhaps, and converses with his thoughts, but there is no person he can turn to if he has doubts or questions. He has become a mirror reflecting what others or a faceless society wants of him. He is vulnerable to being pulled in any direction at all by any random force. One day he strongly fancies himself one way, and the next day he reads or hears something and goes the other way. He is like a boat adrift without an anchor, buffeted by the wind and subject to the whims of the waves.

Long periods of unabated suffering can especially make any man ponder the arbitrary nature of fate and futility of his existence. Whether the suffering is in the form of chronic pain or illness, tragic misfortunes and personal losses, strained relationships and broken families, or from a life filled with abuse, addiction, deprivation, fear, hunger, imprisonment, loneliness, neglect, shame or torture, there are plenty of ways in which simply the act of existing can be miserable. What's the point of it all, he can justifiably ask, if it is so full of meaningless suffering? Yet, even when life is free from all these issues, it can still feel pointless. Being blessed with good fortune does nothing to shield man from the curse of emptiness. If anything, he may feel doubly distraught because he knows he has few reasons to complain.

Great meaning can indeed be found in great suffering. A life lived in the throes of a long struggle has one big redeeming quality. The very struggle that makes the passing moments unbearable can, in looking back, define that life and give it purpose. The catch here is that this sort of meaning is seen only in retrospect.

THE ETERNAL SEARCH

The individual undergoing the suffering does not typically desire or ask for it. A mother who gives up a promising career to stay home and instead take lifelong care of her wheelchair bound, severely disabled child, even into her own retirement years, can look back at her life as having been meaningful, despite the sacrifices. Similarly, the political activist who endures long decades of imprisonment for his beliefs before being vindicated, the impoverished refugee who survives years of working menial jobs while attending night school to finally emerge as a highly respected lawyer, the musician who weathers a long battle with cancer to then produce his finest work yet, all can derive a deep sense of pride for their toils. Needless suffering of an extreme sort, of course, is to be avoided. If man can escape that kind of suffering, it is his imperative to seek out that betterment. Unavoidable suffering, on the other hand, grants meaning to life, but this is a matter of fate. One does not ask for it, nor seek it out.

Viktor Frankl, whose quote opens this chapter, survived several years of imprisonment in a Nazi concentration camp. The list of daily horrors included cruel beatings, arbitrary and brutal punishments, endless hard labor in the cold on meager rations, fettered sleep in rat and flea infested huddles, slow deaths by starvation and disease, and summary executions on a whim. One not only stood helplessly as witness to the senseless deaths, but also had to participate in the dirty work in order to save one's own skin. As the years went by, there was no redeeming event on the horizon to hang one's hopes on. For all that the prisoners knew, each one of them would stay in the camps for as long as it took until they too were dead. Hanging on to life seemed utterly meaningless in these conditions. Yet, those who survived, those who did not fall into complete apathy about their own fate and the fate of others, dug deep to find some meaning even amidst all the meaningless suffering.

Meaning

Viktor understood that even in the most dire of circumstances, man perseveres by creating his own meaning out of literally nothing. Perhaps one man hung on to life because he sought to apply all that he had learnt through his hardship to later become a better husband or father. Another man may have burned with desire to dedicate the remainder of his life after release towards preventing such horrors from ever happening again. The prisoners at the Auschwitz camp defied their SS guards by inverting the 'B' on the sign that they were made to install above the main entrance gate proclaiming 'Arbeit Macht Frei' or 'Work will set you free'. That small act of defiance meant a lot to them. Viktor himself may have wanted to survive past the deathly concentration camp experience so that he could live to tell this truth to the world, that there is meaning even in suffering.

What if there is no great struggle accessible to man that defines his days and gives them purpose? Where does he go to find meaning then? The question especially torments him in this fortunate era, where he has a general expectation of enjoying freedom, safety and wellbeing. The answer remains that he must create meaning in his own mind, but the way he does this in practice is by looking to the external world to show him the way. Those with faith may take a God-centered approach, where they find meaning in their belief, and choose activities that promote and propagate the word of God. Although their belief is largely self-contained, they do rely on the external world for validation, especially if they serve others as part of their faith. Those who lack faith must find purpose in extrinsic ways, in how they relate to the world and the world relates to them. They could find purpose in their relationships to others, such as rearing kids with devotion, taking care of dependents, supporting a partner, teaching, or mentorships. They can also assign meaning to the pursuit of self-oriented goals, such as wealth, power, and creative accomplishments.

Most extrinsic means of deriving meaning eventually run into a problem. Man cannot control his fate or the world around him. Sometimes, the things he has worked on all his life, simply fall apart. One can lose all that one cares about overnight. His loved ones can ditch him or die, his fortunes can disappear overnight, his fame and reputation can be ruined in an instant. Or, he has an epiphany, and his guiding mantra over the past years eventually falls flat on his own ears. He may have worked all his life to achieve a certain form of greatness and one day he realizes that it is all for nought. When the edifices he has built in the world or in his head collapse, when things that he had attached importance to washes away, everything loses meaning with it. The book of Ecclesiastes are the musings of Solomon, a great king of Jerusalem, as he nears the end of his life. He had all the imaginable riches in the world, he had beautiful gardens, he ate delicious foods, he enjoyed a harem of wives. Yet, in the end, he confesses his indifference to these things, and expresses his frustration at the meaninglessness of it all.

Intrinsic sources for meaning stand firm to support man even if everything else outside of his mind has been stripped away. When he asks what is the meaning of life, he may be tormented at not being able to come up with a precise answer. Yet, the act of asking fervently implies that the question must matter greatly to him, and hence a meaningful life must matter proportionally. The question itself then provides the answer. In this manner, even if the meaning of life is nothing, the mind can create meaning out of nothing. Man is not like the lichen on the surface of a rock that exists without enquiring why. Man is not like the deer that chews grass on a meadow without restlessly introspection. Man interrogates himself constantly, which proves that his life matters to him. Seeking a meaningful life is what gives life meaning.

Meaning

Life's responsibilities, the joint pressures of work and family obligations, especially when the demands get intense, certainly make man question things, but these need not detract from a meaningful life. if According to the Bhagavad Gita, the nitty-gritty of his life, the things he does daily, all his actions, his profession, the things he does to fulfil his duties and obligations, these constitute his Karma. This could be wholly different from the why of his life, his goals and aspirations, his beliefs and guiding principles, something that he is always slowly building towards, his lifelong striving, which is his Dharma. Meaning can still be preserved in doing whatever he needs to do to survive and thrive, but yet constantly and relentlessly building towards something larger that aligns with his core principles.

As long as man values his life and the lives of others around him, he will keep asking himself the question of what it means. This is precisely why he derives so much purpose from helping others. Superficial attempts to ingratiate oneself by providing help do not satisfy him because he fails to delude himself. Every so often though, he has the opportunity to truly alleviate and improve the lives of others. Once he has tasted the experience of healing and helping others, he finds great purpose in this, because by doing so he is attaching meaning to their lives and thus also to his own. On the other end of the scale, a man who has lost all meaning in his own life cannot value it at all. Only when he falls into states of total apathy or indifference does he stop asking the question about the point of life. Such a man will not hesitate to end it all and take the lives of several others with him.

In the end, each man must realize that his one life is his only chance to create value with. Every day, he has a choice to make, and that choice is to take full responsibility for his situation in life, no matter the circumstances. When man takes responsibility, he focuses on what he can do, not on what all is wrong with the situation. Taking personal responsibility requires that he stop blaming other people, that he stop finding fault with his setup, and that he stop holding the world responsible for his troubles. After all, he alone is responsible for improving his situation, no matter how dire it is and how he got there. To do so, of course he must engage with his surroundings, put his short life's energy to use, and make just one small improvement each day. This is the essence of a purposeful life.

When the tormented man stares into the abyss and asks of the darkness what is the meaning of life, he cannot hear anything in reply but for a deep and abiding silence. Like the cold, matterless, and immeasurably vast empty spaces between the galaxies, life itself is absolutely devoid of inherent meaning. Meaning exists because he thinks about his life, he finds it worth living, and then he acts. It's simply and solely what he makes of the act of living that gives life meaning.

Community

Anyone who has no need at all for society must either be a beast or a god.

- Aristotle

People who smile while alone used to be called insane, until we invented smartphones and social media.

- Mokokoma Mokhonoana

Picture a gathering. Family, extended family, friends, friends of friends, not friends but not foes either, vaguely familiar faces, maybe some strangers too. Perhaps it's at a courtyard, a square, a town plaza, a park, the village commons. There's kids running around, there's youth huddled in tight groups, there's adults mingling, there's old folks in chairs. It could be there's a party happening, it could be an event, or it could just be a regular day. Nobody was invited, yet everybody is there, since where else would they go but where everyone else is. Some work their trades, some work the crowd, some perform a service, some roughhouse, some observe and soak in. There may be music, there may be singing, there may be dancing. Some prance about, some stand and watch, some clap, some turn their backs. Some eat, some smoke, some drink, some talk, some just listen. There's humor, there's laughter, there's rancor, there's discord, there's sadness too. Something is celebrated, something is mourned, something has changed, or everything is the same as always.

THE ETERNAL SEARCH

There's the same old, there's the new new. There's constancy, there's chaos, there's life.

In contrast to this picture, man increasingly spends his time alone, by himself, isolated, floating adrift and anchorless without a single someone or something to hold fast to or else be the rock for. While the seconds of his life tick by, he is driving the roads, staring at the back of other cars, staring at screens at work, wandering the fluorescent lamp lit aisles of vast markets and malls, ignoring the similarly distracted and avoidant strangers who walk past him, staring even more at screens while in bars, cafes and restaurants and finally the streets, and then driving back home to hear the silence rendered by the hum of his household gadgets, until finally climbing into bed and staring at screens one last time before falling asleep by himself.

Once upon a time, a mere few hundred thousand years or so ago, man was mostly indistinguishable from other fauna that walked the land with him. Then, something sparked in his neurons, something that unleashed the power of his protobrain. He learnt to talk. Now he could share ideas, he could plan, he could learn, he could teach, he could build communal knowledge. The spark grew into a raging fire that outpaced and overwhelmed every other species that roamed the planet. No powerful creature could compete with a tribe of humans, individually weak yet unstoppable when working together. As long as one stuck with the tribe, depended on the tribe and defended the tribe, his kind flourished. All men are all descendants of those that walked that line. Those exiled from the group simply could not make it for long before succumbing to predation, starvation, disease and death. The primitive may not have lacked anything in his life, but he certainly lacked the option of a life outside the tribe.

And then, civilization happened. Modern society has perfected the art of making man exist as a solitary being. Most often, he need not depend on anyone for his survival or wellbeing. With rare exceptions, he is self sufficient. He does not normally starve, nor does he lack any material goods. A different kind of poverty afflicts man now. What he lacks now is the constant companionship of his lost tribe. Yes, he can order food from the safety of his house, entertain himself as he pleases, and earn a living without interacting with anyone. He can live by himself, and he can die by himself. Yet, this condition of isolation isn't entirely of his choosing. Why am I so alone, he wonders. Perhaps there must be something wrong with everyone else, he thinks, for not acknowledging his presence on the planet? For not being able to recognize his qualities? For not wanting to be at his side at all times? How did he end up like this?

Disconnection is both a central consequence and a cause of modern man's obsession with his own happiness. How it became a consequence of his drive to be happy is easy to see. For the primitive, life in the tribe required shared work responsibilities and a commitment towards the common good. Then civilization happened, and man no longer needed that tribe and its obligations for survival. Civilization took care of his primary needs of nutrition, health and safety. He could be independent. First he quit the tight-knit tribe of interrelated nomads, then he left the village where everyone knew everyone else, then he shook himself free of that big extended family, and now he seeks to disband the small nuclear family too and simply live by himself.

Family is everything, agrees everyone. A family consists of a group of people united by marriage or blood or adoption into a household. It is one of the smallest yet also one of the strongest form of communities. Even if all the members don't always live under one roof, what makes a family a family is the strength of interpersonal ties. Family members place a great deal of significance on their relations with each other, such as the bond between a mother and her child or between siblings or between a married couple. Yet, over the last century, the importance of the concept of family has degraded in two key ways. One, many men and women never create family units in first place. Increasingly, they may stay single all their lives, and never have children, or they may have a child but outside of relationships, never joining with the other parent. Two, whatever family units do form are less tightly bound and tend more towards dysfunction. Each member lives disconnected from the others in separate rooms, buries himself or herself all day in some form of cheap entertainment, keeps separate mealtimes, and pursues a completely separate agenda from the others even while existing under the same roof.

Happiness for man has become having a tight set of family and friends, but in another city, country or continent, where they can be reached by virtual means. Certainly not right there in the same house where he lives. He does not need to trouble himself with other people, and their inevitable issues and problems. He prefers complete freedom from dealing with other people's shit. Modern life even provides him with entertainment options that far exceed what another human being can offer. A cursory glance at flocks of gathered humans in a public place such as a park or a train station confirms that he strongly prefers to entertain himself with a screen rather than talk to others. Furthermore, the screens that compete for his attention evolve rapidly to get even better at entertaining, while his human companions remain stuck at the same place. He and his machines interact with ease, and he spends a lot of time doing so. Of course, all this came at a heavy price, because at the end of the day, he is left alone.

Once he has succeeded in totally isolating himself, then and only then does man realize his mistake, in the silent moments between the ticking of the clock that sounds so loud in his empty dwelling. Frantically, he seeks to correct course. I guess I need people in my life to be happy after all, murmurs his rational side. I'm lonely, wails his emotional side. I deserve to be happy, goes another part of his distressed brain. He tries to fix things by doing what he thinks will make him happy, but instead chooses the very behaviors that trap him in a cycle of alienation. When feelings of loneliness hit him at the end of the day, he is tired and can't think clearly, and he says to himself that he deserves a little joy. So then he sits down on the couch with some alcohol or a tub of his favorite ice cream, and turns on the television while he surfs the internet.

The primitive could not obsess about his own happiness because he was tightly surrounded by a close knit group at all times. In any tribe of a few dozen or a hundred odd individuals, young and old, it was a plain statistical fact that there would always have been somebody or the other in the tribe with greater suffering present, up close and palpable. In this situation, he would find it hard to complain about his own trifles. He could not fret about his own minor misfortunes if a member of his tribe lay deathly and feverish from a septic wound that had spread infection to the blood. Someone else would have always been crying out in grief or from childbirth pains or due to other forms of misery. His own happiness was rarely a thing that he could devote much attention to in undiluted fashion. In contrast, modern man can put his happiness front and center in his thoughts. There is nobody else to worry about, and nobody else is around to care for him. In being alone, he obsesses about his happiness alone.

Yet, there is such a thing as the others being too close. Man has forever been caught in the horns of that old dilemma, whether to engage with society, bend to its rules, and tolerate its insults, or to strike out on his own terms and create an alternate life in isolation. In his prehistoric past, he may have chosen a self-imposed exile on occasion, but had no option to return back to his tribe if he wanted to survive. The problem facing him today is that each of his fellow men is an irreverent and incorrigible individualist, like him, and places his own needs above that of the non-existent tribe. Once he has tasted the freedom to do whatever he pleases, he does not easily return to a communal existence. Consequently, he finds spending extended time in the company of others with whom he shares responsibilities and mutual obligations to be jarring and obnoxious. He demands to be compensated if he spends the hours of his day in such cooperative endeavors, which is essentially work.

What about friends? Surely, man enjoys spending time with them, since there is no obligation? Indeed, having a few close friends is essential to his happiness. A true friend is there when needed the most, when he is at his lowest lows. Yet, in the modern version, friends are the last remnant threads of what was once a thickly woven fabric of interconnectedness. Rather than having a few close friends close by him, his numerous distant friends are fragmented across different spheres of his life, such as neighborhood friends, work friends, former colleagues, people he went to school with, people he used to be romantically involved with, sports or activity friends, friends of family members, and random connections from chance meetings. While there is diversity in these sources, the different spheres of his life typically don't mix. They must be dealt with separately to avoid private and embarrassing aspects of his lives from spilling over.

His friends are also often spread out far and wide across neighborhoods, cities, countries, and timezones, which prevents him from engaging with them deeply. He must engage one on one with each of them in order to keep the mutual relationship alive. Mass broadcasts on virtual platforms to large commingled groups of friends are cheap and easy, but these do not sustain relationships precisely because they are cheap and easy, and come across as self-serving, attention-seeking behavior. Engaging in person with a friend, whether for activities, conversations, or companionship, definitely carries more weight, but this takes time and effort. Given the constraints on both sides, he and his friend keep each other at a distance, and fail to develop deeper connections. They selfishly limit what they invest into the relationship in proportion to the benefits they think they can extract out of it. Depending on who is perceived to be at fault, they may feel guilty or resentful or both, for rescheduling or cancelling the plans they make, for being unable to find time for each other, for ignoring each other, and eventually, for letting a promising friendship wither. In the wake of endless such failed dalliances, man grows bitter and sulks. Fed up with wasting his time on flaky friends, he resolves to simply be alone. At least he cannot fail himself, he thinks.

Solitude is the state of man being intentionally alone, of seeking privacy and seclusion for the sake of sanity and reflection. Periods of solitude are not in opposition to or incompatible with a communal life. He has always sought out solitude when people annoy or disappoint him, or when weighty decisions confront him and force him to ponder. Solitude is even a natural response to the chaos of life, where the senses are assaulted to the point that one cannot even think. An occasional walk in the woods or an excursion in the wild gives him new perspectives. When he traverses a vast desolate plain or contemplates alone under the infinite stars, it calms his soul. He forgets his petty troubles when his true insignificance is laid out against the immensity of the universe. This is not to say that such solitude rests easy with him. It is a testament to the strength of his internal fortitude if he can stand to be alone in the wilderness for a few days. When there is no other person or thing that can distract him, he has no choice but to pay heed with honesty to the questions that inevitably arise in his head.

THE ETERNAL SEARCH

What modern man experiences as an accompanying emotion when he suddenly finds himself alone is not the calm of solitude, but the restlessness of disconnection. The quiet simply triggers feelings of alienation. Rather than invigorating him, time spent by himself distresses him. He desperately avoids even the mere idea of having to spend a few hours by himself without distractions. Far from being the lone wolf, that free spirited individualist who wanders miles away from his pack and roams the desolate range in search of something, he is instead like that pet dog that has been left alone too many times and goes berserk at the first hint of enforced loneliness coming his way. In response to this threat, he seeks out cheap distractions, which is the easiest way to fill the gaps of silence. He also makes noise on social media to draw attention to himself. Finally, he calls out indiscriminately to his virtual contacts, his purported friends that always exist somewhere in the ether, yet are never physically present just when he needs them.

Having a community to rely on can heal man of his pain. Not everyone craves this form of healing though. Some, especially those who voluntarily choose solitary pursuits, undoubtedly have a genuinely lower need for social interaction. This may be because they carry a strain of self-reliance combined with traits of introversion. In contrast, there is that kind of man who is actually needy, but he feels awkward or uncomfortable in groups and thus shuns the company of people. He does indeed need external support for his mental health, but is unable to secure it. If he has no friends, then his girlfriend, wife, or even his children will bear the brunt. He can't rely on his own emotional strength, he can't spread that burden around, and so he constantly leans on the one or two close people in his life, often draining them emotionally in the process. In this manner he may push away the ones who he is most dependent on, leaving him completely stranded and desperate for any form at all of human interaction. The best course for him is to force himself to go out and meet people, and try to find a diverse community, so he can safely share his thoughts and hear those of others.

Primitive communities ranged from a few dozen to a few hundred individuals. In contrast, in any large metropolis today, man is surrounded by others numbering in the millions or tens of millions. Yet paradoxically, he has never been more lonely. Every big city dweller knows this feeling well. His condition is like that of the shipwreck victim, adrift on a raft with an entire ocean of water around him that does not quench thirst. Instead of close interaction with a few very familiar faces, he handles tens of thousands of indifferent non-interactions all day with people he has never seen. He takes care to avert his eyes from these strangers even as he sits next to them in a train or walks past them on a busy street, and they do the same. Anyone attempting a smile or a nod is met with awkward surprise or a sullen stare in return. This sort of dance must be conducted from a safe, mutually understood distance. He dare not get too close to the others, for he has grown to fear and detest the smell and touch of other humans as unnatural, unhygienic and unwelcome. His main diversion is to flit between the contacts on his digital devices, making fleeting conversation here and there as time permits. Only rarely is he able to commit to being together with that person face to face, in a relaxed and unconditional manner.

A strong community is essential for keeping malevolence under control. The primitive was always dependent on the tribe for his survival, so he conducted himself well and kept his aberrant behaviors in check. Anyone caught consorting with an enemy tribe, not sharing food from a hunt, bullying the weak, freeloading, or engaging in other such behaviors was swiftly dealt with. The others would band together against him and hand out his punishment, perhaps even exile or death, for threatening the tribe's existence . Most prehistoric societies also conducted initiation rituals to allow new members to demonstrate their allegiance to the community. A youth maturing into manhood or a new entrant into the tribe would have to undergo ritual suffering, such as walking on coals, piercing their skin with skewers, or withstanding long confinement in isolation, in order to prove their worth. These rituals were important because they emphasized the eminence of the group over the individual.

Today, man can live as an island, isolated from all others. He can exist without talking to a soul. He can stay confined to his home indefinitely. He can use apps to outsource his needs for food, transportation and other essentials to strangers that he will never see again. This lack of social interaction allows deviant tendencies to grow unchecked over months and years. If he happens to be slightly unhinged, he can swing out even more on a limb without anyone knowing. Since there is nobody to tell him that he is being crazy, the loner madman's increasing disconnection from reality cannot be curtailed by external feedback. Without intervention, a deranged individual can develop his full delusional potential, till he barrages upon the world with acts of breathtaking evil. Neighbors interviewed by the media about the serial killer living in their midst next door always act surprised as they mention that he so seemed polite and that he mostly kept to himself. Of course he did. The breakdown of communal ties is directly responsible for much evil in society.

Social contact isn't an optional need for man. It is as critical for nourishing his mind as food and water are to his body, even if the effects of social deprivation are harder to see externally. Solitary confinement is one of the most cruel punishments that can be inflicted upon him, and he emerges from long periods of such isolation as a shell of a human, barely able to relate to himself let alone others. The madness that builds inside of a human head in total isolation demonstrates that a solitary life is in fierce opposition to his natural state of being. Even hermits and recluses have an ongoing dynamic with society occurring in their heads, and their need to interact is strong even if their means of communication are infrequent and unusual. The Unabomber Ted Kaczynski communicated for years with society by setting off bombs, reading newspapers to gauge the public's reaction, and then responding to them with more bombs, letters or manifestos.

Historically, man never hung out exclusively with just other humans. For the primitive, community always included nature and its myriad constituent beings. Life in the wild meant life with the wild. He had no choice in this, for he lived under the stars or in a grass hut, and all manner of insects, birds and creatures large and small made themselves uninvited guests to his home. Whether he went hunting, fishing or gathering, whether he feasted and danced or simply rested quietly at a clearing, there were always other species present. The forests around him were filled with life, countless beings with souls just like himself. He depended on some for his existence, he resented or feared others, but he communed with all of them constantly. He himself was but a small part of nature's perennial community. Surviving artifacts from the era are rich with symbols of animal and plant life. For the primitive, communal life was nature.

Throughout history, man has used psychedelics such as peyote cactii and psilocybin mushrooms as ceremonial hallucinogens, and to commune with nature. These substances heighten his deeper consciousness and allow himself to experience the unity of connections within his own self with all of nature around him. The Runa dwellers of the Amazon forests consumed many such substances. Dogs formed an integral part of their hunting and foraging life, since they could hear and sniff things that humans can't even perceive. The Runa took dogs along on arduous hunting trips into the forest lasting several days. And when they took hallucinogens by the campfire, they gave their dogs some too, which made them howl. This wasn't just so that they could understand the language of their dogs. It was so the dogs could understand the Runa better too. The Runa believed that their dogs had souls, just like themselves and all the forest life around them.

Even when man first began farming, he was surrounded by creatures both domesticated and wild. Whether he cared for them or cursed them for ruining his crop, his life lay centered on the primacy of nature. He spent a great deal of time outdoors, as did his children as they played, for the interiors of huts were dark, unlit and smoke-filled places to be avoided in the bright of day. Not surprisingly, he was adept at interpreting the signs of nature all around him. The calling of the crane meant rain, the appearance of the swallows meant spring, the sinking of the fish to the depths meant winter, and so on. His language referred to other species extensively. He talked to them like he did to other men. He formed strong bonds with them that were memorialized in poetry and song. The shepherd and his flock and Maremma dog, the Bedouin and his camels and his goats, or the Mongol and his horse and hunting eagle, all formed tight companions.

Then man began to industrialize his world. Systematically, he removed nature from his life and his surroundings. He burnt down and clear-cut forests, he poured concrete over soil, he chased after and massacred game, and he poisoned and exterminated any animals that remained as pests. He didn't need nature quite as much any more for his physical survival, and he didn't know how to feed his growing needs without destroying it. Every generation, there are fewer birds in the trees, fewer fish in the rivers, and fewer insects that fly into the windshield, but he doesn't notice this decimation because his baseline for what is normal shifts too, and he can't be bothered to care anyways. Now, that day has arrived when he lives alone in a nearly monospecies world, where weeks go by before he even looks

Community

into the eyes of a creature of a different sort, and he wonders if there might be anything missing from his life. The lack of nature is a gaping hole in his soul, whether he realizes this or not.

Cars are the single greatest invention that have killed communities around the world. Cities, neighborhoods, and living spaces all around the planet are designed around the automobile's needs, which are fundamentally different from the human's needs. Cars need long and wide straight paths to travel fast and far. Humans must steer clear of these paths owing to the mortal danger from being struck by tons of hurtling metal. Even when cars are not being driven, they hog huge areas for storage as parking spaces. All of this leaves behind a terrain barren and characterless, as if razed by a bulldozer. Humanity is thinned out and spread alongside roads, creating large swaths of dead spaces devoid of any buzz or life. Being inside a car changes man too. He usually drives alone, with just the three or four empty seats as company while he goes from place to place. The car amplifies his freedom to travel and do things, but it also increases his feelings of isolation and anonymity. He withdraws into his shell, both literally and figuratively, and zones out as the landscape flies past. Other people cease to exist. It's just him, his car, and the road.

Work today also separates man from a community, by first taking him away from his neighborhood on daily long commutes. Then it acquaints him to a transient roster of colleagues who typically reside far from where he lives, and might leave for a different job any day. Finally, work requires him to perform abstract, highly specialized tasks that bear no relevance to improving the day to day life of his community. When he returns home from work and seeks to relax, he turns on the news and hears about broad global problems that mean nothing at all to him or his neighborhood. If anything local is reported at all, it is either criminal activity, which scares him into staying home even more, or frivolous pieces about some cute furry animal getting stuck in an old lady's chimney and needing to be rescued by local firefighters or other such meaningless trifles. His work bears no relation to his home and to what he hears is happening in the world.

A final nail in the coffin for communities is the internet, ironically touted as a way to connect people and bring them closer. Digital networks create a pervasive illusion of communities that man finds irresistible. He is like that bee that is attracted to all the rich color and promise of a scented flower and fails to appreciate the sticky sap of the pitfall trap beneath it until it is too late. Corporations reap monetary benefits from his continued presence and participation on their platforms. They create the framework for a social network, seed it with influential people, and start recruiting. For any trap to work, a few baits must be placed. All that is needed in this case is for a few of his friends to receive incentives for spending time on the network and divulging the names of others. Man is fiercely social, and he cannot resist trying out the latest greatest thing if his friends are doing it too. He inevitably follows their lead. He fears missing out on all that is happening in his nascent digital community, even if it is created out of thin air. Once he gets entrenched, he finds that it is not really the intimate gathering he had hoped for. His friends brought their own friends, who brought their own friends, and they're all there. What started out as a house party turns into a mob of unruly strangers from across the world. Good friends mixed with weak friends mixed with exes and relatives and acquaintances and strangers and weirdos and psychopaths and that one guy he only knows because he exchanged numbers with him after a car accident.

Eventually, man realizes that the social media community is not enriching his life as he hoped it would, and that he spends too much time on it to the detriment of other activities, including living out his real life. He resolves to quit the addiction. He tries to pull the plug, but like any addict, he never truly succeeds beyond brief periods of abstention. For one thing, over time, the corporations got to know him and his preferences very intimately, precisely because they simply asked him and he willingly told them. Maybe he was lured into providing this information in return for making more virtual friends, which he hoped might eventually convert into potential dates, sexual partners, lovers, employers, employees, or even just actual friends. In any case, the corporation's algorithms know him now, better than his mother or even he himself does. As the algorithms continually measure and refine, they perfect an addiction mechanism so finely attuned to his individual needs that he gives up trying to quit. Besides, all of his friends are incurable addicts too, and it's just a matter of statistics that more than a few of them are always active in the community at any given time when he tries to sit it out. His need for staying friends with them outweighs his lofty and principled complaints about how it's all a trap. The platform just needs to run a campaign of bombarding him with reminders to visit and see what he is missing out on, using his closest friends as nostalgic bait, and he's back in short order.

Here again man faces that ancient dilemma, whether to engage with his community and bend to its monocratic rules in order to gain membership, or to go off and chart his own course. Increasingly, he does not even have a choice. The use of social media based digital identities as keys that grant him easy access to a variety of online tools and records means that he cannot disentangle himself from the digital grid without undue hardship. He needs to maintain some minimal presence online, even if it is an impersonal avatar for navigating the virtual world. His true people are not the faceless millions who reside in an infinite universe, so he should not seek to build a community there. He can find and communicate with them in that virtual commonality, but to form close and lasting connections, he must invite them to his own turf or meet them on theirs.

THE ETERNAL SEARCH

The original path to a community relied on cultivating a tight network of dependencies. Dependency is a taboo word today, but in the past it was the foundation of a mesh of bonds that strengthened over a long period of give and take. The peach farmer invariably grew a lot more peaches than he could handle at harvest, and the pig farmer was in the same situation with his many pigs. It made sense to them to trade a few buckets of peaches for a piglet, and for both of them to be friends with the butcher, and for all three to sit and eat at the tavern run by the innkeeper who took all the extra produce from them. The self-sufficient village was the original tight community that traded amongst itself. Until recently, owning or sharing a stake in a small family business such as a restaurant, a gym, or a franchise provided a means of community building. Global commerce has decimated these groups and continues to do so. This avenue of community building is rife with heartbreak, as business after business shuts down and is forced to let go of lifelong employees who had grown close as family.

Communes are experiments at community building that have largely failed. Leaving aside religious communes, socialist-era peasant complexes, and cults formed around political ideologies or spiritual leaders, what remain today are called intentional communities. These are highly focused, non-hierarchical attempts at community building, with an emphasis on joint decisions, shared living and work spaces, shared burdens for cooking, cleaning, chores and childcare, non-industrial scale production of arts or crafts, and ecologically mindful energy and resource use. They typically consist of a few dozen to a few hundred individuals living on a compound that supports a mix of residential, agricultural and industrial activity. Despite lofty goals and the dedication of its members, most face large annual turnover of residents, and eventually disband after a few years.

Community

On the surface, communes sound like a great idea. There is a sense of shared purpose. There are always others to talk to, to work alongside, and to play with. There is joy in creating a new world together and being productive for the good of all, while participating in wholesome chores such as barn raising, tending to animals, raising crops, crafting hammocks or baskets, and cooking for all. However, life in a commune is not life in a utopia. The feeling of belonging to a community is purely a state of mind, which can exist independent of membership in a commune. Communes fail for much the same reasons that relationships fall apart. Even with a non-hierarchical structure, the members try to control each other. Freeloaders and abusive individuals spoil the dynamic. Nobody likes being told how to behave and how to live. The members resent the bounds that are placed on their freedom. They know that there is a great big world out there, and meanwhile they feel locked up inside an artificially limited world, even if it is a safe world. Given a choice, man always wants freedom and options, no matter if it means that he must leave something behind.

Today, a creative community seeker or builder must recognize this truth. His fellow men have gotten used to not depending on anyone for anything. They are so highly individualistic that they cannot be roped into rigid structures that prescribe chores and responsibilities. He must thus find, recognize, or create opportunities that bring people from a range of backgrounds together based on shared interests. All that is needed is for two such motivated people to get together, decide on a shared basis for the community to exist, and then invite a third. Of course, there are no guarantees for success. Once the spark is lit, the process of community building may catch on fire on its own, or it may flicker and go out like a candle. A community may never display a sign that talks about its existence. It exists primarily in the minds of its members. Communities need not advertise or promote themselves, since they might have neither the means nor the need to do so. Inviting sporadic and indifferent visitors as mere spectators defeats the goal of creating a tight knit place. What it needs to flourish instead is a welcoming, open space, perhaps a park or a quiet cafe or someone's backyard or even a street corner, where the members feel safe and welcome, are encouraged to speak their minds. Eventually, the members open themselves up to being vulnerable, which allows them to step forward without the risk of being shamed to offer their hidden talents and gifts for the benefit of the community.

The genesis of this sort of community can often be a chance conversation about a common issue. Two residents of a neighborhood meet at the crosswalk, and observe that speeding traffic has become a problem on their street. They decide to talk further about the problem, learn that they are both motivated to solve it, given that they have young kids who play near the street. Soon, they bring in a third resident, who also happens to be experienced in writing petitions to the city's planning department. Together, they decide on a signature campaign, and go door to door to meet the residents and gather support. A dozen of them self-organize to meet at a nearby cafe, and decide to attend the next town hall. Someone who owns a van offers to pick up the elderly residents who cannot drive by themselves, and they all assemble outside the mayor's office to call attention to the traffic situation. The city eventually heeds to their requests, installs a few speed signs, and assigns traffic police on patrol to catch offenders. The next time the residents walk down the streets, they wave to each other, stop to chat about this and that, and toss about more ideas for improving their neighborhood. Hereby a community is formed, where previously there was none.

The focus of this sort of community is not on what one should fix or do, but rather on the gifts that each possesses. Let's say one man excels at building big wooden sculptures, and a second

Community

is skilled at attaching neon lights to structures, and a third knows how to obtain permits and keep people safe, and a fourth helps organize festivals that draw big crowds. That was all it took to create Burning Man, a vibrant and spontaneous community before it underwent its inevitable commercial metamorphosis. Each individual in such groups enjoys the feeling of being useful to others, due to a strong alignment between their natural interests and their skill expertise. In contrast, too many of modern society's constructs are focusing on fixing individual faults via a one-dimensional transaction. One pays a doctor to fix body issues, a therapist to fix mind issues, a lawyer to fix legal issues, a plumber to fix pipe issues, etcetera. What man needs instead is a place where he is appreciated for what he can do that comes naturally to him, and also happens to enhance the lives of others.

Throughout history, terrible wars, natural disasters and great calamities have tended to bring people together. The differences are erased as everyone tries to help the other with a shared sense of purpose. In the aftermath of earthquakes, hurricanes, and floods, strangers are seen banding together to rescue survivors, recover the dead, build shelters, and run makeshift kitchens. Hardware and grocery stores stay open to give away essentials for free, while restaurants and clinics operate nonstop to feed and care for the needy. These behaviors are not at all surprising, because man thrives in situations where he can be useful. Hardship doesn't bother him, and on the contrary, he even welcomes it, as long as it gives him a chance to prove himself to his tribe. He can withstand all sorts of insults to his body and soul. He can handle the suffering. What he cannot handle is going through life feeling like he is not needed. This feeling is exactly what went missing in his life when he lost his tribe, and this is exactly what he stands to gain if he joins one again.

There is good news and bad news for man, the social being. The bad news is that the world is getting more disconnected, not less. All the traditional structures that held communities together are disappearing rapidly, and the factors that increase his isolation are multiplying at a breathtaking rate. He is fast becoming the loneliest herd animal the planet has ever seen. The good news is that the situation is nearly as bad as it can possibly get. He is already mostly alone, a party of one, and there is no number below that for him to bottom out at. And his kind of folks are growing in strength. There is a strange sort of togetherness and unity in knowing that all he is not alone in his loneliness. It is better that he is lonely in a world where vast numbers of others are lonely as well, than for him to be that rare lonely person while the others are not. The issue facing all of man today is this global deluge of loneliness, and by recognizing this fact, that he is in the midst of this great calamity that affects everyone, is precisely how he can improve the situation for himself, and for others. All he needs is to get together with a second, and together they can find a third, and that is the birth of their own little community. As somebody once said, friendship is born the moment one person admits the following truth to another. What? You too? I thought I was the only one who was alone.

PART II.

ESCAPING THE SEARCH

I am the happy man
Happy, I am

Then one day
like any old dog
I will lay down
roll a tired eye up
one last longing time
at the graying skies
and die

This ugly prophecy
I know it well, yet
in my heart the blood
churns and boils
and I wail silently
Who, me?
No, that can't be!

And howl as I may
or fervently pray
that I am no
ordinary beast
I foam at the jaw
I bite, I gnaw
and live out my days
gripping tight my various
claims to humanity
and eternity

I am the beast
Beast, I am

beast

/bēst/ Noun

An inhumanly cruel, violent or depraved person

An objectionable or unpleasant thing

An animal as opposed to a human

Death

*Man is literally split in two: he has an awareness of his
own splendid uniqueness in that he sticks out of nature
with a towering majesty, and yet he goes back into the
ground a few feet dumbly to rot and disappear forever.
What does it mean to be a self-conscious animal? The
idea is ludicrous, if it is not monstrous. It means to know
that one is food for worms.*

- Ernest Becker, The Denial of Death

Death destroys a man; the idea of Death saves him.

- E. M. Forster

The solo theater of man's real and imagined fears opens every
night in the quiet and dark hours, as he lies in bed and hears his
own monologue play in the confines of his head. The set list
varies but is still predictable. Featured frequently are worries
about his health, his finances, his family, his relationships, his
career, his guilt, his grievances, and his to-do list. And yet,
missing very prominently and strangely is what should be the
biggest source of anxiety to man, which is the irrefutable and
unpredictable eventuality of his own death.

Why should that be? Why is what ought to be his biggest source
of anxiety so often absent in his thoughts? After all, that one
event trumps everything else, and it could happen the very next

day. Why does he worry about a tough work project or a big car repair bill or a roof that needs mending, when all of these trivial concerns will perish when he does too? Unless he has received a death sentence or a terminal prognosis for a disease which makes his demise very real, imminent and predictable, he manages to ignore the elephant in the room as he tosses and turns in bed, fretting and brooding involuntarily about a million other little things.

Rationally, all men readily acknowledge their finite lifespan on this earth and the inevitability of death. They will smile, shrug their shoulders, and effortlessly toss around expressions such as 'you only live once' and 'we all gotta go someday' to endorse this truth. Yet, their emotional side is completely unaffected by this as they daily go about their busy lives. If they were to truly experience the terror of death all the time, they would be paralyzed into helpless inactivity, and unable to undertake the most basic of tasks such as feeding oneself. Nobody goes grocery shopping right after receiving a terminal diagnosis at the doctor's office. Naturally, evolution did not favor individuals who were rendered so petrified by a constant fear of their mortality as to fail to thrive and propagate. Instead, as the human animal developed a concept of self, it learned alongside to keep its emotions in check on the matter of the death of the self. This glaring silence is a neat trick that everyone is born with, no different from the human ear's adaptation to not be drowned out by the drumbeat sounds of blood thumping through the nearby arteries.

Only when death threatens as a likely and very imminent event does the repressed emotion of his fear of dying rise to the surface. Then, he freezes in terror, he screams in panic, he cries in anguish, he pleads with the universe, he goes into denial, and finally, maybe he falls into a grim acceptance. At all other times, normally, he goes about blissfully unaware and unmindful of the eventuality, even secretly pretending that it does not apply to him. The effect of those suppressed notes play out on man's life like an orchestra that is missing all the bass instruments, and the lack of deeper frequencies is felt in the bones. As Becker's quote explains, man seeks to rise above all of nature and stand out as a majestic, invincible being, forever creating beautiful things and performing wonderful feats. To deal with the threat that death poses to this fantastic image, he increasingly chooses two courses of action, both of which constitute a blatant lie.

Firstly, man elaborately hides his dead. He covers them up under sheets, as soon as the death occurs. He then whisks them off to mortuaries, then to funeral homes, and finally to cemeteries and crematoriums. Armies of policemen, emergency personnel, coroners, and other officials of death arrive at every casualty and converge upon the deceased. Never are the bodies left out in the open and unguarded, where someone might catch a glimpse of the decay as it happens. He calls these rituals as showing respect for the dead, but the dead aren't alive to take offense, so the offended party must be the living. Even though there are many more ways to be dead than to be alive, the average man never sees the varied visuals of actualized death in real life. All he sees are cleansed, sanitized and processed dead folks, who all bear calm and serene expressions on their faces as they lay there in a casket, waiting for the living to pay their respects.

Of course, man can watch all the gore he wants via depictions in film and media, but he usually knows that those are just make believe recreations of the real thing, even if they look very real. The most gruesome of such scenes are still usually eliminated by censorship. And on occasion, when by chance a camera does indeed capture an event of death as it occurs or the aftermath of it, the requirement for censoring out such visuals is even more stringent. Why this must be done is never explained, beyond a vague statement that violence and gore are unsuitable for general audiences. Everyone implicitly agrees that the uncensored visuals would be too upsetting and disturbing to watch. Like a big brother protecting the innocent populace from evil thoughts and influences, society curtials man's exposure to death.

The end result of society's concerted efforts to push away the disturbing concept of death is that a child may mature into a man and then grow old to approach his demise, without ever actually having seen one or knowing how to react to it. He does not know how to handle his own death, and thus neither his own life leading up to it. A refusal to authentically deal with the frightening concept of death leaves him incapable of handling a life that he knows will someday end. This reluctance is seen in how he makes plans to deal with his own corpse. He adopts practices such as cremation, which turn him to ashes, or chooses strong caskets made of impregnable materials and then buries himself six feet deep under a big slab. Even after his death, he tries desperately not to become some other creature's shit, especially not the worms. For what is shit but dead life, of course. His own shit is a strong reminder to him of all that was once alive, and now just stinks and stinks of death. It's no surprise that he covers shit up, he hides it, and whisks it away out of sight, just like he does with dead bodies. As every festival or concert attendee knows, man produces lots of shit and constantly, but this must not ever become visible. His cities are marvels of intricate plumbing, all designed to make shit smoothly disappear, that he notices only when the system occasionally fails. As with shit, he does not like to be reminded that death too is a part of life.

This wasn't always the case. The primitive had no choice but to come face to face with the death all around him. Starting as a child who observed the adults hunt and then as an adolescent who participated directly in the killings, early man saw much death as part of his life. By the time he was a youth, he would have stood witness over the last breaths of hundreds if not thousands of creatures, mostly of other species mostly but also those of his own kind. He would have grown desensitized to death long before he was a grown man, and he would not have thought of it as anything but ordinary. He would see death as absolutely normal in the normal course of survival. Consequently, there would be no lasting trauma or stress associated with his experience of the gruesome carnage. This daily experience prepared him well for his own death, and for the death of those around him. Of course, he still feared for his own life and mourned the loss of others, but he did not look the other way from death. He touched it with his bare hands and looked straight at its eyes. Evidence from tens of thousands of years ago shows that the Neanderthals buried their dead in carefully constructed graves. There were no undertakers around to relieve the primitive of the need to handle the bodies of his deceased, so he did it himself.

For all the centuries up until the last one, there was an obligation for the family of the deceased to mourn while engaging with their dead for as long as was practically possible. The Trobrianders of Papua New Guinea stayed beside a dead tribe member for days inside a hut while they burned coconut oil and incense to mask the smell, and even after the body had to be disposed off, they continued to mourn. Wails of lament, tragic crying, and the many rituals to mark the death went on for weeks. The deceased individual's kin would cease to cook food and instead agree to be fed by the community for this period, while they made arrangements to distribute property belonging to the dead back to the community. The family would also acknowledge the death by shaving off their hair, removing their jewelry and adornments, and dressing in black for as long as they mourned. What is notable about these death rituals is that they were mirror images of childbirth ceremonies, which were celebrated just as extensively as the deaths were mourned. To celebrate the presence of new life, the infant's kin dressed up in their finest clothing and jewelry, prepared a big feast to feed the entire tribe, and the newly made parents now received gifts from the whole community. Similar responses to a new life or a death in the community were common in most primitive cultures.

Modern society has aspired and succeeded in making death less of a downer for everyone concerned except for the one doing the dying. The whole process of dealing with the dead has been outsourced, especially the messy bits concerning the corpse itself, such that family and friends have no obligations except to make some calls and then arrange to receive an urn with the ashes. They may make some public statements about keeping the dead in their memories, but again not for too long. The emphasis for the living is on commemorating rather than mourning the life of the recently dead, and then quickly forgetting in the name of moving on. One gives a toast to the dead man, a few speeches are given with humorous episodes inserted for comic relief, and then the champagne comes out. The partying begins thereafter, indistinguishable from any ordinary party, and justified as a celebration of life rather than an admission of death. With a few notable historic exceptions such as Christ and Kennedy, the world of the living today moves on all too quickly from the events surrounding the demise of the ever growing numbers of their dead.

Aside from hiding the dead and forgetting about it, the other massive effort that man undertakes to minimize death is to invoke a countless series of impermanence projects. He subconsciously knows that he will perish, so he is constantly obsessed with things that will last, beyond him, maybe even forever. He builds monuments, the bigger the better, that carry his name for all to see, for centuries to come. The temples of kings, the pyramids of the pharaohs, and the modern day skyscrapers are all symbols of his wish for impermanence. He creates giant circles in the desert that can be seen from space. He builds dams so heavy that they change the wobble of the planet. He seeks to discover new species, he rushes to be the first to step foot on Mars, he wants to find a cure for cancer. He wants to be known for something, anything, even a horrible crime, just to have his name go down in the books or newspapers for posterity. He gets involved with ideas greater than himself, and hopes to be recognized forever as the creator or the champion of these ideas. He associates himself with great companies, organizations, sports teams, religions and cults, all of which he hopes will outlast him past his death. He idolizes people, things, and ideas, and then he worships these false idols as Gods that will grant him immortality.

His own children are man's most natural of impermanence projects. Unlike other creatures that breed and beget without a plan, he usually enters into deliberate acts of procreation to produce offspring. He can thus claim to have a hand in designing the creation of life itself, and this avenue becomes his grandest endeavor to stave off impermanence. Technology has given man, the conscious animal that abhors its own mortality, further ability to control his progeny. Each of his offspring comes to represent a bit of himself. He takes pleasure in knowing that some of his essence is transferred to the child and survives to be passed on to the next generation. His children are thus his carefully conceived little couriers of immortality into the future, whether he likes to admit this or not. Once he has placed the burden of his own death fear on to his little children, he then protects them far more than is necessary, because they represent to him his pet immortality projects.

The more man is troubled by his inevitable fading away, and the greater his means of acting on his distress, the more he tries to reproduce his way out of trouble. The Mongol emperor Genghis Khan is said to have fathered thousands of children over decades of military campaigns as his armies invaded village after village, slaughtered the men, and raped the women. His direct descendants today are estimated to number in the millions. Ultimately though, no matter how far man goes with this exercise, he fails just the same as if he had never tried. All that is left of Khan's efforts are myriad individuals living their lives oblivious to a core reason for their existence, namely the agony of impermanence faced by a man now long gone and very much dead. And given that they face the same pain as did their ancestors, the problem just perpetuates forward with each generation.

Man's obsession with stuff also reflects his desire for impermanence. He likes to collect attractive goods of a non-perishable nature that keep for a long time. Things that were never alive or are already dead by definition won't die with him, and by owning these things, he hopes to share in their permanence. It's no surprise that goods marketed to him frequently make claims of their longevity far past his lifetime, which he then values beyond reason. A diamond is forever, gold never rusts, and the marble flooring will last him for generations. The well known problem for him here is that after a lifetime of accumulating durable objects, he still can't take anything with him when he goes. Still, he can't resist the endless acquisitions. He especially likes buying land, as much as he can afford and far beyond his needs, because he then owns that piece of earth for eternity. The larger the patch of ground is, the larger he presumes his legacy to be. He forgets that all he will ultimately need is something in the proximity of six square feet. That is, if he prefers to be food for worms. Less still if he chooses to be dust.

The most original and least imaginative impermanence project that man pursues is, of course, actual immortality itself. He has always sought to break free from the natural bounds on his lifespan set by biology or fate. The quest for living in eternity, or at least with a greatly expanded life expectancy, has been his dream since time immemorial. Whether it was the ancient Qin dynasty emperors who pushed a thousand alchemists to concoct an elixir of life and eternal youth, or the aging billionaire today

Death

who invests his immense wealth into life extension technologies, man often reaches a juncture in his life when he realizes that everything he has achieved in the physical world counts for nothing when the clock runs out. He will die like everyone else, taking nothing along.

The more wealthy, powerful or accomplished man thinks he is, the more he feels he has to lose when he dies, and his natural tendency is to fight this inevitability tooth and nail. Such a man believes aging to be a disease and considers a natural death to be an unnatural event. Logically then, the solution to the problem of death is to attack it head on with all available means at his disposal. He tries all manner of drugs, supplements, therapies, modifications and replacements to try to stave off the inevitable. Corporations lure him and his money with the tantalizing promise. Their siren song always goes that if only he could just make it as far as when technology has advanced to the point that true immortality is finally achieved, all will be good. After all, it would be such a crying shame if a man of plentiful wealth and means died just a few years short of when the possibility of extending his life by decades or even centuries became a reality.

For the most part, these are empty promises. There are a million different little bits and pieces that make up his complex body, and a billion different ways for these things to go wrong and malfunction. The chances that his technology will be able to simultaneously stretch the life span of all of his body's component parts by a significant amount are probabilistically slim. Nevertheless, he may try and he may even succeed, but he still cannot claim to escape death completely. Leaving aside the practical issue of bodies eventually falling apart to disease and decay, there is also the issue of plain mishaps. If he expects to live not a hundred years but a thousand years, then the threat of a sudden and unfortunate death looms even larger each time he simply crosses the street or goes for a swim in the ocean or flies on an aeroplane. He can then also expect to spend many days being paranoid about this fate, avoiding any risk and all those cruel random twists of fate that may shorten his entitlement to a quota of a long life. In other words, he is doomed to live a life devoid of fun. No amount of tinkering and tweaking and patching to extend life will change this fact.

To technological mavens, impermanence is a concept that can be conveniently be distanced from the physical body. Such men hold the belief that with the aid of surrogate bodies of thinking machines, their consciousness can live forever. From the viewpoint of these modern voyagers who seek to transcend time, the human body is clearly a messy vehicle to live and travel within. It suffers from pain, it frequently breaks down, it decays, and eventually it rots. The focus of the believers here is on a concept they call singularity, whereby their thought processes and mind states can be transferred to a computational machine, thus leaving behind the limitations of a perishable body and soaring into the ether forever. Even if such a feat were possible, it is never clear who is this person or thing that now lives in the ether, and whether its clone mind is merely an imitation replica of the real. The mind that was left behind in the flesh and blood version meets the same fate as ever, and its magnificent stores of memories start to muddle and fade mere minutes after the last breath was taken, long before when the brain matter starts to go sour inside the skull.

Romantic relationships are another common area of striving for impermanence, with the end result being a great deal of interpersonal strife. Every love affair starts out by man elevating the object of his love to a sort of Goddess. She is his savior, because she covers up his flaws. If he dislikes some aspect of his own appearance, personality or history, then her fabulous looks, charm or pedigree can make up for that. He claims to have found someone perfect, not just in absolute terms but especially

Death

for him. Even if she is imperfect in some manner, those quirks are initially categorized as delightful and heavenly. Together, he thinks, the two of them are destined to be eternally happy in this state of perfection. He wants this blissful union to continue forever. Of course, things change over time. People change, they evolve different needs, they age, and they show their flaws. He does not like any of this. He tries to control her, and he does not permit her to change, he prevents her exploration. He wants her to be with him, as always, forever. Of course, she resents all of his attempts to control her, and runs from him. He first creates a Goddess out of his woman, but then when she rejects him or fails him, he hates her for shattering his concept of a permanently blissful relationship, and seeks to destroy her. This is the personal brand of evil that manifests itself commonly as jealousy, anger, and violence between former lovers.

All of these attempts by man to secure permanence constitute a gaping hole in his grasp of the truth. He displays a remarkably persistent unwillingness to acknowledge his mortality. He is constantly in the state of what Ernest Becker called a denial of death. Man's fervent denial of death is the source of much evil in the world. He starts out with good intentions but then puts too much effort into trying to hold on forever. He treats people around him, his loves, and even his own children, as pawns in her personal quest for eternity. He refuses to accept his limited time allotment and ravages blindly through the world like a madman, building ever bigger edifices to himself, and proclaiming to the world that his creations will last forever, when nobody will care in a hundred years time and even if they did, he won't be around to see them care. In the process, he destroys much of what is good around him. The vast majority of needless suffering in this world is self-inflicted, if not by man on himself, then by man on his own species.

ESCAPING THE SEARCH

The denial of death occurs at three levels simultaneously - personal, interpersonal, and societal - and that is also the order in which the denial crumbles, if at all. Scenes from Leo Tolstoy's The Death of Ivan Ilyich vividly illustrate this. Stricken by an incurable disease, the formerly powerful magistrate Ivan lays dying slowly in his magnificent room, wasting away over a period of several weeks. Prior to his ailment, death to Ivan was an abstract concept, something that happened to all men of course but never truly applied to his own case with any real weight of emotion. As his disease progresses inexorably, he still on occasion comes up with reasons to deny the inevitable, but these self-delusions are less effective now. He accepts his fate, if unwillingly. He then starts to get increasingly annoyed at his wife, his friends, and his doctors, who drop by his room for sporadic visits, almost in passing, before running off to a party, a show, or some errand. It irritates him to see how they all cheerfully pretend that he's just under the weather for a bit, and will eventually regain his health if only he would stop complaining and just stick to his regimen of diet and medications. He resents them for continuing to maintain that lie of things as normal. Only his son and his servant show tears to acknowledge the truth. His greatest resentment though is reserved for society, as he hears the busy streets outside his window, people driving places, playing music, drinking, eating, singing, and going about their lives as ever, oblivious to his plight, as if nothing would ever change for them, as if they themselves would never die, even as he now lay dying.

Death denial builds up in man from an early age. When a toddler starts to pay attention to his image in mirrors and see himself for who he is, he has formed a concept of self. Further understanding then slowly trickles into his expanding conception of the universe. Perhaps he comes upon a dead bird in the grass, or he pushed a stick into a bug and the bug stopped moving, or somebody in his family circle passes away. He asks a few questions and he receives some unsatisfactory answers, but slowly he puts a picture together of how all living creatures must do this thing called dying, after which they don't move any more. Still, he is only vaguely aware that he himself will one day die. Perhaps as he gets older still, he witnesses an accident or has a near miss himself, and as his heart beats furiously, he realizes that it could have been him dying. Fortunately, nature equips him with the ability to disconnect his rational and emotional sides in order to cope with this very disturbing thought. By the time a child is able to speak fluently, he has fully incorporated the knowledge that all living things must die, but he is complicit with the adults in generally being silent on the topic and unperturbed by it on a daily basis.

As he enters his teenage years though, a rebellion develops. Where previously he was silent on death, now he taunts it, he toys with the concept endlessly, and is fascinated by it. Across cultures, teenagers develop and display a peculiar obsession with death and its symbols, such as zombies, vampires, mutilated bodies, bloodfests, massacres, violence, and gore. They seek out movies, images and stories that pander to their morbid fantasies about death in all its forms, despite the attempts of society to hide them from it. Adults may vilify the teenager for his abnormal fetish, but this brief phase in fact represents the last burst of honesty that he will experience. Before he goes into full denial, he may attempt to convince himself that he is above death's reach. He taunts mortality by engaging in risky and dangerous activities, purely for the sake of thumbing his nose at it. He adopts a shield of invincibility that allows him to embrace this death defying behavior, which serves to push the fear of death further and further away. Dying is something that old or sick people do, he thinks derisively, and since he is neither old nor sick and he doesn't fear it either, he is safe. He may even believe just a tiny bit that he may escape death altogether, just because he is special and especially robust, and couldn't possibly meet the same fate as those ordinary others.

One day he graduates from his carefree youth and is now an adult. He doesn't taunt death any longer, and he tells himself that this is because he doesn't need to prove anything. He has responsibilities now, and perhaps other people depend on him. He doesn't taunt fate quite as much as he used to, but he still doesn't fully appreciate his mortality in how he lives his life. Every once in a while, he gets an epiphany from a trigger event. The passing of a close friend, a personal brush with danger, or other tragedies serve to temporarily shake him up and remind him to think deeply of matters. He reacts by cleaning up his act, perhaps by cutting out the destructive habits from his life, getting out of addictions, abandoning harmful or unfulfilling relationships, and prioritizing his family and his friends, or his creative passions, over blindly chasing wealth or status. Still, the effect doesn't last, because he finds it discomforting to contemplate his mortality at length. He'd rather stay distracted and oblivious.

Invariably then, he repeats the same mistakes over and over again, potentially all his life, until that day arrives that he never saw coming. It may take him a few decades and a few hard knocks on the head before he finally sees things clearly. Sometimes, this clarity arrives with him receiving news of a terminal diagnosis from his doctor, even if this later turns out to be a false alarm. He then walks around in a daze for days, feeling like he is stuck in a bad dream, and unable to comprehend how everyone else around him can laugh and carry on as normal when he will soon be dying. At other times, the realization that he will cease to exist comes out of nowhere and catches him unawares. It is as if one fine day, a crack suddenly opens in his solid conception of himself, and a blinding light filters through. He acts as though he is finding out for the first time that all men are mortal, himself included. He was so used to experiencing the world from the point of view of that conscious being that lives inside of his head, that the idea that one day this viewpoint itself will disappear is just incomprehensible, even stranger than the whole world itself ceasing to be. The shock of the episode knocks him flat for weeks or months. He loses interest in all other things as he grapples with acute anxiety and panic caused by his emotions finally acknowledging what he has rationally always known to be true. As opposed to an existential crisis, which is a case of being troubled by the question of how to deal with one's life, this is a crisis of non-existence, or how to deal with one's death. He may never go back to being his old self.

Yet, the nostalgic pull of that blissfully ignorant state which existed prior to the shock is strong. He desperately wants to regain his carefree former self. He wants to pretend that his episode of existential shock was a glitch. He chides himself for brooding on negativity, and as he looks at other people going about their lives in unperturbed fashion, he once again persuades himself back into denial. Many years may pass again while he dives into distractions and shelters himself inside various projects. By this time, he may be truly old and nearing the end anyways. The aged cannot but be aware of their mounting physical limitations and declining health, and they receive frequent reminders of their coming fate from the passing of friends and relatives in a similar age group. Still, a few old men will never exit denial, and remain immature on the topic and behave accordingly for nearly the entirety of their lives. Their acceptance of mortality and their regret for having prioritized the wrong things in the past comes when their ability to change the path of their lives is limited. Old age is no time to begin the difficult process of accepting that one is going to die.

In the meantime, while he is still in denial, the evil that man does is in direct proportion to his inability to see that it is the fear of his own mortality that drives him to go to insane lengths to compensate. After all, what are the world's greatest atrocities, genocides, criminalities, mass executions and wars but attempts by the evil doer to build up some grandiose impermanence project. Take as an example the Colombian billionaire drug lord Pablo Escobar, regarded as the wealthiest criminal in history, and estimated to be responsible for killing over 5,000 men, women and children, including 107 innocents in a passenger plane bombing. Escobar's vast network produced and distributed cocaine in such large quantities that he ran out of physical space in his compound for all the incoming bundles of cash. He resorted to stashing piles of cash in Colombian farming fields and warehouses, and was reportedly resigned to having to write off ten percent of his money each year to rats and mold. This was not a man doing what he did for more money or what that extra money could buy him. The reason he could not stop is that his grand project had taken on a life of its own. The immense and intricate drug network that he had created seemed to him far more enduring than even his own life, which he knew could end at any time in a spray of bullets, as it eventually did.

The world has seen endless cycles of brutal genocides, with the death toll running into several tens of millions. Hitler's Holocaust exterminated six million lives, Pol Pot's Cambodian genocide claimed two million, the Rwandan massacre of Tutsis killed one million, and the list goes on. If one includes the toll from ill-conceived economic and social campaigns, the final tally grows staggeringly larger still. The Great Leap Forward in China led by Chairman Mao is estimated to have resulted in thirty to fifty million famine deaths. Stalin's Five Year Plan took five to ten million Kazakh and Ukrainian lives. Large calamities continue to happen in parts of Africa. A notable feature of such tragedies is that they invariably result from cultural and societal reform movements led by hardworking and motivated idealists. Once the idealist has envisioned his version of utopia, it must be brought into reality at any cost, since it forms his claim to eternal fame. All manner of atrocities are then justifiable as simply small and necessary steps taken towards a great enduring future. If the idealist becomes obsessed with the idea of improving a nation, then eliminating an entire race of supposedly inferior people becomes a trivial technical detail. He has attached himself to a grand idea, and simply cannot let go, even if it comes at the price of the deaths of millions. Of course, much good and progress also arises from the same force of idealism, of man torturing himself to do something special that he believes will secure him immortal fame, but he cannot make progress on eliminating evil until he sees his true motivations.

Death acceptance is the only cure to the pervasive problem of death denial. To rid man of his denial and the evil that originates from it, the Buddha recommended meditating on death itself. Theravada Buddhist monasteries display images of decomposing corpses, so that monks can contemplate the finiteness of their bodily selves. The Stoic philosophers of ancient Greece recommended a daily practice of envisioning new and novel ways in which one could meet one's end, as a means of cultivating death acceptance. Society today would commonly regard such practices as morbid and abhorrent, but that is precisely because death denial is very deeply ingrained in man's psyche and culture. Shopping complexes, malls, stores, restaurants, bars, sports and entertainment venues, television, social media, news, games, etcetera all benefit from a certain mindless consumption that is a lot easier to encourage when the customer is in death denial. The unwillingness to confront death facilitates the smooth functioning of society and lubricates the gears of the economy.

The practice of meditating on one's own demise is difficult to perform with genuine intention and dedication. The average man will suffer from great anxiety and distress when he tries.

Thinking honestly about his own death literally crushes his every dream, ambition and hope, at least during the initial phase of acceptance. It goes against the grain of everything he has learnt from a culture that prides itself in covering up all scenes of annihilation. Thoughts of death tend to be incompatible with the pleasurable feelings associated with indulging in wealth, power, beauty, sexual conquests, material goods, and other impermanence projects. Of course, this deprives him of pleasure from his favorite addictions, and he misses those from time to time. Periodically, he is tempted to revert to denial, since mindless pleasures can only be enjoyed when he wanders aimlessly from day to day, amusing himself with this and that.

It may take a few challenging months or years before he gets comfortable with simultaneously holding the idea of death as a constant companion to his other thoughts.
Yet, if he persists, if he endures his distress, he exits successfully into a state of death acceptance. The idea of death sharpens his focus and purpose, and cleanses his mind of its tendency to seek distractions. Difficult as it may be to continually maintain, a gentle yet constant meditation on his impending and unpredictable death rids man of a great degree of anxiety and evil. When he has the idea of death frequently in his mind, over time he grows calmer about the ups and downs in his life. Once he gets used to the idea of his own mortality, he paradoxically fears it less by a gradual process of desensitization. Repeated exposure to scary things makes them seem ordinary and normal.

And death is indeed normal. It is also very ordinary, despite the extraordinariness associated with it from being hidden and suppressed. It too is a part of life. In a state of death acceptance, man is thus more in touch with reality than he has ever previously been in his life. A closer alignment with reality brings his frivolous, mindless and destructive behaviors under control, as his thoughts are guided away from grand delusions of

Death

permanence. His attention sharply focuses on what will matter to him most when he dies, on what he finds meaningful, on how he can make the most of his short time on earth, and on whom he wants to share this time with. He wants to make every day matter, and spend it meaningfully in pursuit of his true passions and with those that are his true loves. This is the reason for the truism, that although death eventually destroys man, the idea of death will save him.

Birth

After your death you will be exactly what you were before your birth.

- Arthur Schopenhauer

Birth and death are two aspects of the same state..

- Gandhi

For much of human history, childbirth was an unadulterated horror of an ordeal, for mother and newborn alike. The setting for the delivery might have been a secluded spot in a humid forest teeming with wild animals, or a hammock inside a dark and smoky hut, or perhaps just a suitable patch of flat vegetation by the side of a trail. Depending on the era and its conditions, the mortality rate for the infant was as high as one death for every two live births. For the mother, aside from the horrendous pain of labor, there was the frightening prospect of dying from placental hemorrhage, seizures and organ failures, bacterial infections, puerperal fevers, excessive bleeding, post-labor complications, and plain old starvation. Her risk of death from each childbirth was maybe a couple of percent, but given that she gave birth to ten or more children over her lifetime, the chances of dying added up to be pretty high. The average primitive woman had a coin's toss chance of making it out alive from running past the gauntlet of endless childbirths that she endured. Even in the middle ages, a woman tended to take out a will as soon as she found out that she was pregnant. Clearly, the enormously sized brains of the human primate species have come at enormous costs.

Coincident with the long and dark history of birthing were women's attempts to take control of their bodies and their involuntary string of pregnancies. The only reliable yet daunting avenue of contraception available to the primitive woman was to nurse the last set of infants as long as possible, since breastfeeding suppressed the hormones she needed to get pregnant. Every few years though, she would be able to conceive again, in an endless cycle that would continue for decades until her body was physically unable to bear births. Lacking the means to control births, many of the offspring coming into the primitive's world would have been viewed with relative indifference, perhaps even as unintentional or unwanted products of sexual relationships. This isn't to devalue the mother's immense love for her children, of course. That bond is one of the strongest found in nature, and intensifies even more over time as the child matures. Yet, a dual love-hate nature was always present in the mother-child relationship, perhaps even more so than it is today. Their battle for supremacy and control begins when the newly formed embryo releases its hormones into the mother's body to shape it to its needs, and the tussle continues past birth as the newborn constantly demands the nipple, and then resists being weaned for years. Every successive birth pushed the primitive woman to the very limits of what she was willing to sacrifice.

Not surprisingly, the terrors and travails of childbirth have always inspired a wide range of drastic preventive measures. The history of abortion is almost as old as the history of conception. A short list of the various pre-modern methods employed to induce an abortion included fasting, bloodletting, subjecting oneself to a beating, tightening a girdle, application of pressure to the abdomen, strenuous labor, overheating oneself, enduring stabbings or crude surgical excisions, and the consumption of poisonous herbs, leaves, or heavy metals. The death rate from attempted abortion was as high as one in three. In other words, historically, women frequently chose a relatively high risk of dying from an attempted abortion rather than undergo the ordeal of delivering another unwanted birth.

In addition to the sheer physical agony of labor, the primitive woman also endured one of the most intensely raw psychological ordeals found in nature. To feel and see her body being literally ripped and torn apart from within by this other little human is to encounter feelings that have no parallel in the human experience. Even if she survived the event, she would have come as close to dying as one possibly could. Then there is that weird bisection associated with birth, where a part of her own body, something that has been inside and growing inside of her for nearly a year, is now pushed out as a separate thing. Even if she rationally knows that this slimy bundle of living flesh is not part of her anymore, parting with it does not come easy. With each successful birth, new life is created outside of the woman, but something equivalent must cease to exist inside of her, for what is outside now is clearly not inside her any more. Something dies when something is born.

If a man were obliged to have to give up say part of his spleen or a kidney of his, and further if that organ had a mind of its own and decides that it wants to grow within him for a few months, getting inexorably larger and larger, and then to secede from him by simply tearing away and exiting with a flood of blood and fluids through an orifice in his lower half, and if the man were forced to endure this as it unfolded slowly, painfully, with waves of cramps lasting several hours or days even, all the while lying helplessly in a soaking wet puddle of his own making, while dozens of random folk play spectator, gape at the widening hole, offer a variety of advice, attempt to speed things along, and then celebrate it as a personal accomplishment when they finally pull the slimy and bloody thing free, then he can get some sense of what was typically involved with natural childbirth.

A definition of the female of the human species then is the gender that is physically and psychologically capable of enduring the death of a significant part of herself to create a new life form, and to potentially face complete death herself in the process. Every woman is born with this innate capacity, and every man is not. The idea of life and death comes more slowly to males, through external means, from his experiences. He can only take lives, as many as he wants, which he indeed does on occasion. Rarely, he can save lives, such as when he rescues another human from certain death. Still, he can never create life from within. Man does what he can to feel powerful, to exert his influence over creation and destruction, and if one cannot give, one is obliged to take. The woman has her inherent capacity to bring new lives into being, and these are her universally recognized, all important keystones to claim significance with, if she chooses to. The man has no such thing to claim as his. Perhaps this explains why he tends to play with his own life and risk those of others, to commit murder and homicide, and to take lives out of the world with such greater relative ease.

In contrast to natural childbirth as it existed for eons, the common modern spectacle of a sedated, pain-free, managed delivery in sterile conditions, at a conveniently scheduled hour, with half a dozen strangers administering drugs, anaesthetizing the woman, slicing open her belly, extracting the baby, and sewing her back up, seems laughably mundane. It is a both a miracle of modern science and a gross travesty of the extraordinary event that marks the creation of new life. Both the infant and the pregnant woman often miss out on the hearty screaming and thrashing and blood-splattering drama, and then a gloved nurse hands over the stunned newborn that got rudely yanked out into the open to the equally dazed and confused mother or the helpless bystander father, and informs them that this is their little baby, and they did it. All the focus is then diverted to commercialized rituals celebrating the new arrival, such as baby showers, gender reveal parties, and the choice of the exact pastel shades for the walls of the baby's room.

Even in today's world, nearly half of all women will have undergone an abortion at some point in their lives. Furthermore, roughly half of all pregnancies that are carried to term are still unintentional, either due to accidents, one- or two-sided failures of contraception, forced intercourse, or intercourse while intoxicated. Not surprisingly, the emotions surrounding a pregnancy at the time of its initial discovery are often very different from the glorious welcome party it is made out to be at the time of delivery. Society generally celebrates a birth, no matter why life came into shape inside the mother, and in complete disregard to her private feelings about the events leading up to it. The process of birth also allows for the slate to be wiped clean as the infant exits the birth canal. It doesn't matter if the father was a serial killer, a terrorist bomber, or a dictator who raped by the thousands, like the Dominican president Rafael Trujillo whose squads roamed the night streets of Santo Domingo, looking for young girls to bring back to El Jefe. The sins of the father fade away in the womb. The child is always innocent. No matter the tortuous path to existence his life took and the drama it entailed, the child does not ever choose to be born, nor does he select the circumstances of his birth.

The child then always comes into a world not of his choosing. Man has a biological drive to bring children into the world, yet if all the grown children were asked for their opinions on the quality of their existence and choose again, a lot fewer might be born. As the philosopher Nietzsche told it, to live is to suffer. It is not hard to justify this position. Much of life is a struggle, and some lives are clearly so full of misery that one can argue against the point of such an existence. A majority of individuals born into the world will suffer from a combination of conditions such as neglect, hunger, thirst, poverty, lack of shelter and sanitation, inhumane living conditions, abuse, torture, slavery, disease, chronic pains, alcoholism, drug addictions, and mental health issues. Unfulfilled desires, loneliness, and strife are common circumstances in almost every man's life experience. Even for a largely good life, there is always a shadow cast by the ever present threat of disaster and ruin. And every life always ends the same way, with old age and disease leading to an eventual demise, or the tragedy of a sudden and unforeseen death.

It has also been rightfully pointed out that there is a great asymmetry at play between positive and negative states for both mind and body. Suffering is generally present far in excess of enjoyment. The body's potential for pain is far greater than its potential for pleasure. Any doubts about this asymmetry can be quickly dispelled simply by making the rounds of any hospital ward to talk and listen to the chronically sick. Pleasures tend to be fleeting and limited in intensity, while pain can be long lasting and seemingly unlimited in intensity. Given a choice, no man would choose to experience the best of pleasures for a certain period of time in return for having to experience the worst of pains for an equal duration.

Every day it seems, life brings a new issue in front of man, and these challenges tend to present themselves with greater frequency than items that are good news. There are unpaid and unexpected bills in the mail, there's a new and nagging swollen lymph node that is worrisome, there's something his partner or parents or children have done that requires fixing, someone close to him is very sick, the engine on the car is making an ominous sound, the garden sprinklers have stopped working, the pet dog has been throwing up all the food it eats, the project at work ran into a block, the airline arbitrarily changed the flight departure time and now he will miss his connecting flight, etcetera, etcetera. Every event adds a new fold to the fabric of his already very crumpled universe, and as time goes on, everything in his life gets more complicated, not less.

After all the trouble involved in coming into existence, if that existence itself is such a painful struggle, then why does man persist in existing? Why doesn't he just resort to throwing his hands up and admitting to his miserable condition, and then simply let himself waste away? The simple explanation of course, is that he is unable to do so because of the tight control that his biology exerts upon him. Evolution has programmed him with a tenacious drive for survival, and he is compelled to persist and procreate in spite of mostly not enjoying the overall experience. His greatest attachment is to his existence itself, and he fights to retain his life despite it being largely unpredictably and even unpleasant for long stretches. Life may be undeniably tough and wretched, but no matter how hard it gets, the human animal hangs on resolutely. For the most part, except for the rare acts of suicide, he is remarkably resilient and durable in the face of suffering. The way nature tricks his psyche to hang on is by making him two things simultaneously. He is a die-hard optimist, and he is a talented illusionist.

Optimism comes naturally to man. It is his deep default state, even though he doesn't realize it. At a basic level, he always expects to wake up the next morning, make it till the end of the day, wake up the morning after that, and so on, even though these events are completely outside his control. Even a so called pessimist, who frets about bad things happening to him on a daily basis, largely still expects to survive into the next day so he can experience his proclaimed worst case scenario and be vindicated in his beliefs. He expects to have food to eat, water to drink, and for life to go on. Even when those essentials are at risk, in the direst of circumstances, man will still retain the tiniest amount of hope that his condition will improve and that he will regain control over his future. Of course, each time he gets buffeted by real or imagined misfortunes, it lowers his outlook on life until he finds a way to bounce back. These mood swings happen several times a day, sometimes every hour, as he rides a wild rollercoaster of hopes soaring and plunging and soaring again at the slightest of provocations. Nevertheless, since he always retains some hope, and hope applies to the future, he will always hang on to see what tomorrow brings.

Delusions of grandeur are the other means by which man convinces himself to keep going. He deceives himself on a massive scale about his own uniqueness. He is like that masterful magician who creates a dazzling performance with smoke and mirrors and diversions and distractions, all of it for an audience of one. Himself. He has an amazing repertoire of cognitive fallacies that allow him to retain a high opinion of himself, relative to others. The average man fervently believes that he is above average in every respect, despite this being a statistical impossibility. He is more kind and considerate than others, he works harder than most, he is a better driver than others on the road, he is more dedicated as a parent than most, he deals with life's circumstances better than the average person in his place would be able to, and so on. Occasionally, his high opinions get dinged and challenged by encounters with external opinions or facts, but he quickly finds a way to recover. For instance, if a man values himself for being rich and successful, and he then discovers someone even wealthier in his circle of friends who makes him look poor by comparison, he quickly consoles himself with a variety of thoughts, such as how he is kinder than that other guy, or a better looking man, or a more authentic human, and so on. His high regard for himself is dynamic, opportunistic and resilient. No matter what, he is a unique and valuable individual. And if this is the case, he reasons, then surely his life must be worth continuing, irrespective of the circumstances. He must endure, through the ups and downs.

To combat the pain of such a volatile existence, the Buddhists proposed the concept of Shunyata, which translates as nothingness or emptiness. This emptiness isn't that negative emotion of feeling apathetic, or what one refers to as purposelessness. Instead, it is a neutral meditative state where one realizes that the feelings, desires, judgements and emotions associated with life's moments are an illusion, based on human cognition assigning subjective qualities to phenomena. If one watches a video of a man fuck a woman, how he feels about it depends on whether the man is his neighbor and the woman is his wife, or he is simply watching strangers in a pornographic movie. If a bar of soap makes one tear up, it could be because the scent reminds him of his ex-lover, or it could be because that was the same brand that he bathed with every single day for ten years while in prison. Observed natural phenomena themselves have no emotional qualities attached to them. It is man that forms the emotions. If he strips away the attachments and the accompanying emotions, what he is left with is Shunyata, the nothingness, which is nothing but the objective, observable universe.

Here is the story of Buddhism in a nutshell. A long time ago, in a place called Lumbini in the northeast of ancient India, a prince named Siddhartha was born. His circumstances were so privileged that as he grew up, none of his needs ever went lacking. Yet, as the prince traveled outside the palace grounds, he saw past his own sheltered existence and realized that suffering was widespread and prevalent across the world, no matter where one looked. Siddhartha eventually realized that this suffering arose because humans get attached to things they crave, such as riches, power, stuff, youth, beauty, lovers, and their own lives. They get entitled to these things and want to acquire them and possess them permanently, but since all things in life are fleeting and ephemeral, they feel the pain of unfulfilled desires and the fear of impermanence. Siddhartha devoted his life to teaching this wisdom, for which he gained renown as Gautama Buddha, or 'the enlightened one'. His wasn't by any means a unique realization. Ashoka, the emperor who conquered everything and then wept, or Solomon, the king who had every pleasure he could wish for and yet grew dissatisfied, and numerous others have formulated the same concepts, although nobody has expressed it as eloquently as the Buddhists.

The Buddha's advice to man fundamentally comes down to the following. Don't play games that you cannot win. If life is a roulette wheel of sufferings and mishaps, then to stop being attached to outcomes is the best course. As well known is this advice is, and although everyone occasionally experiences it as an epiphany, the spark of wisdom doesn't last for long. The simple fact of the matter is, most men aren't saints or enlightened beings like the Buddha. The average man automatically and unconsciously forms attachments to everything he touches. Furthermore, his opinions on how to live are strongly influenced by society, which reinforces his craving for things like money, power, fame, beautiful lovers, and an eternal life. His culture pushes back at his attempts to be indifferent to attachments and outcomes, and it takes an exceptionally strong internal culture to resist the pressure. And if he is to engage with the world, and not become as indifferent to everything as a hermit, then he has to participate in some game. He must choose some aspirations to devote his time and energy towards attaining. What can the average person do then to escape the cycle of getting attached to his aspirations and then continually being disappointed? How can he secure his happiness?

The fact that man can ask this question of himself, and then tries to answer it with more esoteric reasoning, itself illustrates the problem. In contrast to how modern man thinks, consider how the primitive might have gone about it. Objectively, all the big questions of life and death, these were all the same then as they are now. The biology of their brain matter is unchanged. Yet, their perspectives are worlds apart. Given a raven, a lion, a snail and a yam, and then asked to pick the odd item out from the group, modern man properly identifies the yam as the only item of the four that belongs to the plant kingdom. The primitive though wouldn't hesitate as he picked the lion, since that's the only thing out of the four that he would immediately run from. The difference here is one of living in the abstract versus in the experiential. Primitive man made decisions based on his direct observation of the world, and while this limited him to immediate and easily accessible concepts, he was firmly grounded on his personal experience.

Modern man, on the other hand, persists in a wholly different state of mind. He is influenced heavily by indirectly learned concepts. He can theorize and hypothesize endlessly about all manner of things that he has no deeper knowledge about except what he has heard or read. He can assert with confidence that the Big Bang theory explains how the universe began, yet he has no clue what he means. He is just repeating something from somewhere. His knowledge is impressively broad yet superficial. He is fine trusting the experts when they tell him that the earth is a spherical object that rotates on its axis, even though his personal experience of observation strongly suggests that the earth is flat and stationary, and it is the sun and the moon and the stars that move through the sky in circles around it. Of course, the experts are often right, especially if there is scientific evidence backing their claims, and then his belief in them is justified. The earth is indeed round, and the sun is indeed the center of the solar system. At other times, there is zero personal or scientific evidence, yet he blindly believes what society at large tells him to believe. His conviction that happiness is something that can be actively pursued in order to secure it, is one such unsubstantiated truth.

In theory, modern man is convinced that if he finds and then follows a certain prescription for life, that is all he needs to do to be eternally happy with his lot. He is solution oriented and driven to fix issues, and his happiness is one such issue to be fixed. In practice, since he cannot consistently be happy given life's vagaries, he therefore chases after the concept of eternal happiness even more furiously, and gets increasingly frustrated at its elusiveness. In this way, how strongly man goes about trying to secure his happiness has no bearing on his actual happiness. On the contrary, it makes him unhappier still. The more he can't have it reliably, the more he craves it. This is the essence of the problem facing him today. A thousand books have been written all claiming to bestow lasting happiness upon him, and yet none will concede that perhaps this permanent state is inherently unattainable. Never will it ever be admitted that the very act of laying down a brightly lit and well marked path to the lost city of happiness renders it as an unattainable destination.

The history of happiness worship is coincident with the history of languages, and especially with the origin of the written word and its ability to influence opinions. When man began to put his thoughts down in writing, he could formulate new and abstract concepts and use them to affect the thoughts of others. With the word of God serving as a guide and a prod to action, he was convinced to abandon the forest, then work in the fields, then work in the factories, to acquire money and goods, to seek power and fame, and to worship certain people and things, all in the name of eternal happiness. Once his happiness was proclaimed as a desirable yet attainable state, it got elevated as an ideal to be pursued by all. Man's pursuit of happiness is duly enshrined in religious texts, in revolutionary political manifestos, in the constitutions of nations around the world, and most recently, in the advertising campaigns of large corporations. Every organization or entity that wants to sell him on something starts by first telling him that he deserves happiness, and then offers him helpful ideas on how he can attain it. Human happiness is an easy target for the largest sustained campaign of psychological manipulation that the world has ever seen.

Compared to modern man, prehistoric man was a more impressive physical specimen overall, with much sturdier bones and construction. Similarly, when it comes to mental health and robustness, modernity has left man frail and weak. The signposts were put up pointing the wrong way, and led him down a disastrous route which emphasized blind positivism over realism. Pop-culture philosophy promotes the claim that all that is needed in the face of life's challenges is simply buttoning down with a mantra of cheerful thoughts. Prescriptions for mental wellness include such activities as forcing a smile when standing in front of the mirror, repeating upbeat commandments to oneself, or thinking of a minimum of three good things a day. The average person then walks around with a cheery mask held steady for the external world, no matter how he feels on the inside, since he has incorporated the message of positivism to mean that his facial expressions and demeanor must not reveal his true inner turmoil. In other words, he must pretend to be happy in order to be happy, which is a nonsensical piece of logic, of course. This faked happiness just encourages superficiality all around, prevents honest reflection, and gets in the way of meaningful corrective action. The continual charade serves nobody well, yet everybody persists in keeping up the pretenses.

Men will live out their whole lives often without ever having accepted life for what it truly is. Entire decades of existence can be spanned without a single moment of realism, because genuine realism is harder even than simply putting a foolhardy smile up for everyone to see and carrying on. Of course, not every man is able to delude himself like that for long. Here and there, one of them cracks under the strain of life and breaks from the ranks of the pretenders. When he does this though, when he finally drops the pretense and abandons his act of cheerfulness, he does so with a vengeance. He goes under a dark cloud of depression, or he explodes upon the cheery world of other pretenders in a destructive burst of evil. Colloquially, he is said to 'go ballistic' as he snaps and unleashes his pent up anger. A common characteristic of many a mass shooter is his admission that he fantasized about ripping off what he believed to be masks of happiness from the faces of his victims. To validate as normal his own feelings of darkness and gloom, he wished to see the smiles disappear, especially from the faces of all those happy pretenders.

The happiness fetish goes into overdrive when mixed with modern superstition and mumbo-jumbo. Some men have been deluded into thinking that the external world can be impacted purely by thoughts alone. Enigmatic concepts, marketed under authoritative names such as the Secret Law of Attraction, trap gullible men whose yearning for happiness overwhelms all critical judgement. By simply thinking positive thoughts and desiring something strongly, so the logic goes, the object of their wishes will be attracted to them. For instance, one could get rich simply by thinking intensely about wealth, or win over a lover just by engaging in focused brain activity that imagines a life with that person. This is utter nonsense, but the lure of wishful thinking is strong. The result is a widespread and obsessive focus on things that one believes one needs in order to be happy, accompanied by much fervent wishful thinking. Eternal happiness is the nirvana of this new religion, and 'because I deserve it' is the mantra one repeats to get there.

Man needs instead to revert to practical realism. The primitive was an uncompromising realist. If a creature fails to feed or drink or generally act in accordance with its needs, it does not survive long. This was life for the primitive. He satisfied his daily needs with his own labor. When faced with an issue, he fixed it if he could. If the infestation of bugs in the thatch of his shelter became unbearable, he had to tear or burn the hut down and build it anew. If he was running out of food in his belly, he had to leave camp and hunt or gather. He did not stand inside the hut and chant about all the things that he was thankful for in his life. Nor did he read self-help books that asserted with circular logic that he could achieve anything at all that he wanted if he were to just want it bad enough. He didn't have gurus and motivational speakers telling him that everyone deserves to be eternally happy, and this ideal is within reach. What served him well in every situation was exactly what he needed to do to fix the situation. Mundane realism. There was no need for positivism or wishful thinking as preached by some invisible societal voices.

Life acceptance is the purest form of realism. It begins with man acknowledging that his existence will almost certainly face all sorts of struggles, and it concludes with him taking full responsibility for improving his situation. Acceptance is not the same as resignation or the act of giving up. Nor is acceptance to be confused with suppressing one's complaints, colloquially known as a call to 'suck it up' and 'deal with it'. There is no self-delusion at play with acceptance, where one tries to control one's mind and think only positive thoughts. Man can't ever not think of something, especially if he is told not to think of something. Accepting his condition and his thoughts about it is a necessary first step to actuate change. With that done, he can take onus for fixing issues where possible, instead of hiding from them or assigning blame on others. As per the concept of Shunyata, how he subjectively feels about an objective fact comes down to his own judgement, so the responsibility for changing how he feels also falls upon him. He must put in relentless effort. This may or may not improve things, but the striving gives purpose to his life. This is realism, as opposed to expecting only the best for oneself and then continually being disappointed. Or, expecting the worst yet doing nothing at all to prevent it, thus fulfilling one's own prophecy. Life acceptance is thus neither blind positivism nor cynical passivism.

Acceptance need not leave man all somber and cheerless. On the contrary, it brings a smile to his face, except that this is not that fake smile that one pastes on as a public pretense. A recognition of one's true place in the universe brings with it a realization of how laughable the whole concept of life really is. The philosopher Albert Camus wrote that humans should embrace the absurd condition while defiantly continuing to strive and create meaning. The purpose of life is a purposeful meaninglessness, a truly ridiculous state. To laugh at someone else's misery or misfortune is the fastest way to lose their respect, yet by the same token, to be able to laugh at one's own misery or misfortune is a universally admired trait. It shows that one has eyes wide open, yet is not taking himself too seriously. This is the definitive response to accepting life, because to be able to laugh at it shows that one has no pretences. Acceptance is thus aligned with being aware yet cheerful in the face of harsh reality. Ultimately, the greatest gift man can give to the people in his life is to be joyful in their presence, without pretense.

Acceptance brings practical benefits to all spheres of life. As an example, an obese man may be avoiding true acceptance in a misguided pursuit of happiness. He may tell himself that simply by imagining himself thin, he will get there. This sort of wishful thinking is futile, of course. Or, he may fake acceptance and say that it is okay to be obese, and that it is society that should accept him. That stance puts him in constant opposition both to a culture that leans contrary to this, and to his own wishes to be healthy. If choosing passivity, he may just shrug indifferently and say that there's no point in trying at all any more, because he's far too overweight now, and anyways he does not care, which again is not the truth of the matter. Rather than fighting the actual weight problem, he ends up spending his mental energy fighting the messaging problems he has created in his mind by deviating from realism. Instead, if he were to simply acknowledge without judgement that he would be better off by losing even a bit of weight, he can then devote energy every day to exercising and eating better. Over time, he can make small progress on weight loss. This builds his confidence in his ability to influence his own life, while simultaneously improving things.

Similarly, someone caught in a deteriorating relationship can pretend that everything is okay, or he can blame his partner, or he can choose to try to fix it. The choice is his, and the responsibility is his. Ignoring the issue with mere optimism and positive thinking allows the unhealthy relationship dynamics to persist, and ultimately leads to a blow up when a trigger is found. Cynicism, contempt, or playing the blame game does him no good either. His only real choice is to accept that the relationship needs to be fixed, and begin to make that improvement. He must engage with his partner, discuss what both need to do to address problems, and take small steps along those lines. Of course, there will be situations when small steps aren't what is needed. If things are broken far beyond repair, then the only course is to exit the relationship. Even this requires acceptance that things have ended for all practical purposes. In the absence of realism, he stays hanging on long past he should. Acceptance provides the clarity needed to move on.

Life acceptance energizes man into action, once he realizes that it is all up to him. The results that he seeks are by no means guaranteed, he knows that fully well, but it is up to him to try. His world might be fucked up, everything may be going to hell, and he may justifiably feel like shit about all of this. All that does not matter. The only question is, what is he going to do about it. This is the true reason man should be relentless in the face of life's challenges. Not because he thinks he will attain some abstract happiness, but because every challenge is an opportunity for him to prove that his life is worth living. This is how he prevails over the voices of learned helplessness in his head, that say to him that it's no use trying, or that it's not his fault, or that everything will be fine if he just thinks positive thoughts.

The greatest tragedy about coming into this world is that man cannot observe his own birth, which is the most singular event in his life. Every child listens with rapt attention to stories about the events surrounding his own birth, yet he can never experience the miracle of his own creation. At some period while growing up, the child develops a full sense of self, and from that point on, he acts entitled and takes his existence for granted. It is as if he was always present. He finds it hard to believe that there was ever a time when he did not. If he were a formless spirit with a mature consciousness prior to his conception, such that he could experience his coming into the physical world, first inside his mother's womb and then through the birth canal into the open, he would regard the event with much greater respect and sense of gratitude than he normally does. As Schopenhauer and Gandhi have told it, he would see that what he was prior to birth is the same as what he will be past his death. A uniform state of nothingness.

At the beginning of time, there were a trillion possibilities where the universe could have collapsed onto itself before it originated. There were a trillion ways in which the galaxy that holds the sun could have not formed. A trillion things that could have gone wrong before the planet that is earth came about. A trillion permutations existed for the basic molecules of life to combine into something other than primordial cells.

ESCAPING THE SEARCH

A trillion alternative histories can be narrated where the simple life forms did not survive catastrophic events and extinctions to evolve into his human ancestors. And finally, a trillion factors were stacked against his particular genes coming together in his mother's womb. Each wailing newborn is an astoundingly unique life form, an incomprehensibly improbable statistical fluke. As the only conscious being on earth, man has the unique gift of knowing this. He is aware of the miracle of being, even if he doesn't fully appreciate it. It is completely up to him then, how he chooses to celebrate and immortalize that short period of existence between two very great eternities of nothingness, which is his life.

Rebirth

Man's main task in life is to give birth to himself, to become what he potentially is. The tragedy is that most of us will die before we are thus born.

- Erich Fromm

The sun must set to rise again.

- Robert Browning.

One day you came into this world alone, naked and covered in slime, perhaps splattered with your mother's blood, urine and feces. You don't remember anything about this event. And one day you will die and exit this world alone, and turn to mud, dirt or dust. You won't remember anything about this event either. All the interesting stuff in your life will happen between those two forgotten events. There are no two ways about it, for anyone. No matter who they are and what they do with their short time on earth, the book of everyone's life story has those exact same first and last pages.

Every night you go to sleep, and it is a bit like getting to die in miniature. When you wake up in the morning, you have a chance to be born again, but day after day, you let that chance slip. You misread the same maps, you chart the same wrong paths, you end up at the same dead ends, and at the end of each frustrating day as you crawl back into bed and lay your weary head to rest, you wonder where your life took a wrong turn, and why. For you to experience being reborn, for a part of your life to begin afresh, a part of the old you must die. This is the part of you is that contains your hidden belief in your impermanence, and the implanted opinion that your happiness is a concept to be chased after and caught.

Just be happy and think positive thoughts, that is the commandment you always hear. As if it were the simplest thing ever, to keep all of your wandering thoughts fenced up like cattle on just the grass is greener side of the meadow. Wait, you say you aren't happy, and your thoughts aren't all positive? Then just chase after whatever will make you happy, comes the response. Well then. What all can one chase after, in that pursuit of happiness? Money, women, and status? Do whatever makes you happy, they say. How about if you do meth or armed robbery? What if those are the things that happen to give you your kicks? Your primitive ancestor could get by just fine if he just followed his survival instincts throughout the day. In today's over-privileged world, if you just did what makes you and just you happy in the moment, you'd quickly end up addicted to alcohol, drugs, food, porn, and the internet. How far will you go then in your selfish pursuits? And at what price? Isn't there a better way to guide you through life, than this perverse and all-consuming obsession with something that cannot be secured anyways? Can you wake up and be reborn as you open your eyes every morning?

You can start the process of rebirth by wiping the slate clean. Too many ideas may have cluttered up your head. Your well intentioned attempts to learn more and more might have been subverted. Everything you've ever heard, everything you've ever seen, and everything you've ever read, whether in the news, in the media, in books, in movies, on television, on the internet, or even from the mouths and words of other people, they're all present there in your brain now and for one primary reason. Somebody was trying to sell you on something, whether some actual goods or just an idea, and for you to take the bait and bite, they probably tied it to a lure of happiness. And so you live your life, pursuing some abstract and nonsensical state of eternal bliss, while being told what will secure that by numerous others.

Contradictory messages on what to do and how to live bombard you from all sides. These have probably left you floundering and confused, going one way one day and another way the next, depending on what you hear and what you read and how they persuade you. Just be yourself, you hear sometimes. Be edgy and be cool, you hear at other times. Get rich, get laid, get hammered, say those who idolize a carefree existence. Actually, don't chase money, don't chase women, don't do drugs, say others who advocate caution. Work hard, that's one piece of advice. Don't work too hard, that's the other piece. Focus on your career, some will tell you. Nah, quit that nine to five and just follow your dreams, others urge. Do one thing really well, some say. Just do all the things in life that you love, say others. It's wise to save for retirement, that's one message. Live a little, cuz what's the point in dying rich, that's another message. Love the one you're with, someone says. Don't ever settle though, says another. Eat this thing to be healthy, one study says. Actually, that stuff is carcinogenic, you read somewhere else. Spend on experiences, not on stuff, one great article says. A well-made pair of leather boots are worth it, says the advertisement next to it. Buying a house is smart, argues one friend. Heck no, just rent and avoid the hassle, says another. Etcetera, etcetera.

All of it is too much information, all of it is someone else's opinion, and all of it is just hearsay. None of it is your own witnessed truth. So shut off the news, the media, the glut of messages, for a day, for a month, for a year, or forever. You've probably heard, seen and read plenty already, more than enough to last you a lifetime. Of course, you might worry about missing out on something important, something that shows you the way, something to get you permanently out of your funk of unhappiness. You might worry that you will lose your way without all these helpful tips. You might worry about turning into an inferior, illiterate, or uninformed human being. You might worry about what others will think of you if you're shut out to popular culture. They might grow concerned that you have become impervious to outside influence, to their opinions. What you might be most worried about though is what you will have to think about if you can't rely on external stimulation. Your life, without the mess of signposts and distractions. Imagine that. Scary.

Once you have done that, once you have emptied your brain of junk facts, you will be ready to replenish it with the foundational axioms that apply to your life. Here then are your experiential truths. Even if these aren't all things that you may have personally witnessed, someday you surely will, or you will witness them in others. One day you will die. It may be sudden and tragic, or you may suffer a slow and painful decay that makes you fantasize about the quick version. On that day, just like any other day, the universe will not care if you live and thrive or suffer and die. Just like you were born alone, you will die alone, because even if you are surrounded by those who love you, they will not be passing on with you. It will be like the sadness of leaving on a long trip, except you're not coming back ever. In the meantime, until that day comes, this is your life to live. There is no other life. No magazine or movie version that you might picture yourself in. No alternate reality to fantasize about or escape to. And the people around you are the people in your life. They are your people, and likely will remain in your life. If you don't like them, you can try swapping them out for new ones, but most likely they are not the problem. Of course there's some good folks and some bad folks, or more accurately they all have some good days and some bad days, but your number one priority has to be on fixing your own faults. The stuff between your ears is your sole responsibility, because nobody else can cure that for you. You can't blame other people for your issues, and you can't control them anyways, try as you might. Try as you might, you cannot control all of life either. Fate will make strange and unexpected plans for you. Hopefully, you are able to tell the difference between what life does with you and what you do with your life, so that you can accept without judgement the parts that you cannot control as the price of existence, and you can accept with totality your sole responsibility for improving the parts that you can control.

In the first half of this book, you read about twelve typical areas of existence where most people attempt to seek happiness. You saw why once you get what you need, the essentials of life, any further attempts to derive more happiness will fail. Your wants are endless, and modernity panders to them under the guise of giving you routes to eternal fulfillment. Your commercialized, unsubstantiated, and esoteric perspectives on life are so different from the direct experience of your primitive ancestors that you have very nearly forgotten how to live well. You are continually led astray in your attempts to follow paths that others tell you will lead to eternal joy. Life acceptance and death acceptance are the only two guiding principles that you need to follow, once you have straightened out all the disarray in your head. Death acceptance allows you to uncover mindless distractions and bring your focus sharply towards what you truly find worthwhile, while life acceptance energizes you to tackle each day as precious and live life to the fullest of your potential.

Both forms of acceptance are crucial for a life well lived. One is no good without the other. They are two sides of the existential equation that you must embrace equally. With just life acceptance alone, you may be striving hard each day and taking full responsibility for improving your life, but your goals might be ill-chosen. You might be stuck in a mindless pursuit of worldly matters, such as spending all your time chasing after meaningless amounts of money or stuff. You need to accept your mortality to realize the meaninglessness of such striving. On the other hand, with just death acceptance alone, you may succeed in cutting out mindless pursuits and destructive behaviors, but you may end up in a passive state of resignation about the pointlessness and absurdity of it all. You will be devoid of an urgency for living and for making things better, unless you accept that your short life is relevant and meaningful only because you strive continually to create meaning with your relentless efforts.

With acceptance of both sorts, you can start living again from scratch, as if it is your first day on this planet. Sure, you may ask, what difference does acceptance really make in the rhythm of the day to day. Let's say that in the short term, you have no leeway to change the fundamentals of your situation. You live in the same place, you go to the same job, you do the same things after work, you live the same life. Will cultivating acceptance change anything here? The answer is a definitive yes. Acceptance changes both your mental state today, as well as your unrealized future tomorrow. Life acceptance changes your perspective on the very same life, allowing you to take responsibility and control over the parts of it that you can change. It allows you to fulfil your Karma. Death acceptance lets you to choose wisely the paths that you will take to shepherd your future life towards greater fulfillment. It lets you find your Dharma.

Primitive man would have found the modern practice of voluntary exercise, such as going on a run with the sole intention of burning calories, as laughably insane. Yet, given the circumstances of life today, exercise makes perfect sense. We have too much junk food around us to consume and not enough physical activity. Similarly, the idea of engaging in a regular practice of life acceptance and death acceptance may seem needless and unnatural, until one considers that we are surrounded by too much junk information to consume, and nearly not enough mental exercise is done to offset it. This is why you must remind yourself daily about your gift of life and your mortal fate, and meditate regularly on these truths to keep them on the top of your thoughts. The following short mantra can be silently considered to mark the end of each day. I accept my life, and therefore I accept my death. I accept my death, and therefore I accept my life. When morning comes, you can choose to feel reborn or you can choose to repeat the wasteful cycle you were in the day before. That is your choice.

For you to truly accept your pending death is one of the hardest things you will ever do. Unlike other epiphanies, whose effect can evaporate over time, once you have fully accepted and ingrained your mortality, it changes your life in a lasting manner. To be sure, it may cause you great discomfort and anxiety, to be thinking about your own demise and impermanence. You might wishes that you could just forget about it all and waste the hours away on one frivolous distraction after another. The fear of non-existence is not the sort of mild anxiety that can be conquered by taking a few deep breaths or downing a couple of drinks to forget things. It is the sort of pain that must be embraced daily if you are to cope with it, because it demands that you submit to your place in the universe. You must face the truth, as much as is humanly possible. You must dare to stare at the sun, even if that blinding light overwhelms you and forces you to turn away.

Consider the following paradox. A judge handing out a sentence tells a condemned prisoner that he will be hanged upon waking up some day within the next week. As a further punitive twist to the ruling, the day of the execution is to be a surprise to the prisoner. He will not know whether it is his final day on earth, until the hangman shows up outside his cell door. Now the prisoner is a smart man. He thinks about his situation, and reasons that he can't be hanged on Friday morning, because the judge had said that it would be a surprise. If he survived his hanging past Thursday, then there would be no element of surprise left in the hangman coming to get him on Friday morning. He then reasons that Thursday morning cannot be when he gets hanged either, because Friday has already been eliminated, and if he hasn't been hanged by the end of Wednesday, then a Thursday morning hanging would be no surprise. By continuing with similar reasoning, he concludes that he cannot be hung on Wednesday, Tuesday, or Monday either. In other words, the hanging cannot occur at all. Overjoyed with this conclusion, he retires to his cell and celebrates with a bottle of moonshine. Then, on Wednesday morning when he wakes up, to his utter surprise, the hangman is standing outside his cell door.

Most of us apply reasoning like that to our lives. I can't possibly be dead by tonight, because I have dinner plans at that Italian place. I can't be dying by next Tuesday, because I have a concert to go to. Next month I'm going skiing, and in a year's time I'll get my business degree. And so on and so forth. We convince ourselves that our lives will go on as always. Indeed, chances are, many of us will live long and into old age. Yet, those golden years may never arrive. Does this mean that you should shrink your horizons and just live for today, since you may be gone tomorrow? One often hears advice to treat each day as if it could be your last. But that doesn't seem right either, and represents the other extreme. If you lived like that, you would never bother to brush your teeth or file your taxes. Not doing such things have consequences and cause suffering down the line, such as major dental problems and jail time for tax evasion. You still have to plan for tomorrow, but live today as if you truly don't know when it will be your last. Unlike that prisoner, you have to be aware that life is not under your control. You cannot apply logic to plan everything out. Learn to accept your mortality, and then you can stop worrying about it and go live your life, instead of pretending it won't happen, but secretly worrying about it all the time.

You cannot secure your happiness in place. Trying to secure it will only make you feel worse, so you should stop trying completely. Forget that there is such a word as happiness. Accept that you will be not happy on many occasions in your life, but those are precisely the times that you learn the most, something about life or about yourself, and grow as a person. Many of the good things that happen in your life might come after you felt unhappy about something and crucially, you resolved to get out of that state. Being unhappy is sometimes the best thing that can happen to you. Sadness too is a part of life. Stop chasing after eternal happiness or peaks of happy experiences, like the kind of things your friends post about on their social media feeds while skipping over all the mundane hours or the really shitty moments. Instead, focus your efforts on connecting with the people around you. Help them with whatever they need that you happen to be good at. Be generous with your time and energy, and spend your resources to bring joy to their lives. That's how you form a little community around yourself. That's how you don't end up all dead inside, completely useless to others and yet feeling sorry for yourself. That's how you regain your lost tribe.

So here's what it all comes down to. You've read this book and you've read other great books and you've read a thousand things. You've seen and heard much. You know all the places where you might have sought your happiness and you know where those paths all led to. They all led back to you. Stop wishing then for some other life, for there is no other life but your life. Start by working on that one. And not with an eye towards some vague future notion of your personal utopia. As forward-thinking animals, we humans like to pretend that we can see the road in front of us, and fathom what lies ahead in the mist for us to blow away and uncover. We're forever trying to get from where we are to where we think we should end up to be all set for life. In reality, we should be standing with our heads turned facing back to where we came from and what we did then. In other words, our own history of actions. The only thing we can see clearly is how we got to be where we are, and what we do now, how we act now, will become your new past and will be the only thing that sets your future. If you think that your life sucks and the world is fucked, and all of that happens to be perfectly true, the question still remains what are you going to do about it while you are still alive.

Here's a helpful analogy to guide your path forward. Imagine a little fish swimming in the vast ocean. Let's say that being close to the blue skies and warm sunlit waters is this little fishy's happy place, while being in the dark, cold and sunless ocean depths is its unhappy place. Naturally, it loves to swim towards the surface, where the golden rays shine through. As much as it wishes for though, it can't jump out of the water into the air and stay up there, of course. All that happens when it tries is that it splashes back in. And tempting as it may be to stay right there, parked with its nose held steady where the water meets the air, that isn't any kind of life. Yes, the dark and cold depths of the ocean are practically bottomless, but that is where this little fish needs to go, like all fish must, to grow bigger and stronger. Those dark and cold depths too are a part of life.

If you truly love someone, you have to let them go free. This means that you don't mind when they wander away from you, and you don't try to obsessively control them. You let them return to you when the time is right. It is the same with your happiness. You must learn to love being away from your happy, sunlit place. You will be a better human when you return to it. No matter what is causing your suffering right now, consider it as a challenge that improves you, and appreciate it for that. You have to remember that when you can't have something that you want, you want it even more, and your inability to attain it frustrates you. And when that something that you want is to be happier, the fact that you want to be ever happy is essentially the cause of your frustration. Give up your obsessive need to be happy, and you will actually enjoy a more satisfying life. Once you stop being attached to a narrow definition of how your life should be, it frees you up to be open to a wider range of experiences. Today, it is a miraculous gift that you are alive. Tomorrow, that may well be the day that you are going to die. And only when you accept this truth in your bones, that you are mortal, can you truly start living. In the meantime, just remember to let your happiness go, and you will be alright.

The right to the pursuit of happiness is nothing else but the right to disillusionment.

- Aldous Huxley

END

Made in the USA
Monee, IL
19 December 2019

19091982R10150